SUPER
CULTURE™

SUPER CULTURE™

---

5 SIMPLE RULES TO CREATE A SUCCESSFUL
ENVIRONMENT AND A HAPPY TEAM

Tony,

Praise What You Want Repeated!

Chris Cornelison

CHRIS CORNELISON

Million Dollar Author™ Press

Dedication

To Janet–my wife, best friend, and biggest supporter, and my kids Alex and Megan. Your love and support are what created this book. Thank you for always supporting me. I love doing life with you all; you make it worthwhile.

To Charlotte and Ricky Cornelison, aka, Mom and Dad, thank you for teaching me integrity and laying the foundation for all that has happened in my life.

To all the many Eagles I have had the honor of working with and building Super Cultures™ and Super Teams, thank you for being the driving force behind every success!

CONTENTS

Foreword

In the world of business, there are visionaries, and then there's Chris. A true firebrand of an entrepreneur, Chris's journey through leadership and culture-building is nothing short of extraordinary. For over 15 years, we've had the privilege of witnessing firsthand his unparalleled energy, a force so vibrant that it doesn't just light up a room—it electrifies it.

His experimentation with the elements of creating a Super Culture™ has turned theoretical concepts into practical, tangible results. He embodies the essence of "walk the talk" principles, making him a rare breed in today's fast-paced business environment. The clarity of his message in this book, distilled from years of experience, provides a roadmap that makes it accessible for anyone who desires to build a Super Culture™.

The old Peter Drucker adage, "Culture eats strategy for breakfast," is one that Chris introduced to us. It's a truth he's lived and breathed, transforming it from a mere saying into a cornerstone of his leadership philosophy. His ability to nurture, grow, and develop other leaders is a testament to one of his many superpowers.

This book is a culmination of Chris's lifelong dedication to fostering environments where culture thrives. It's a blueprint for anyone looking to elevate their organization, to create a space where strategy and culture are not at odds but work in harmony. Through these pages, you'll find the essence of what makes Chris's leadership so impactful and why his lessons are indispensable.

Prepare to be inspired, to be challenged, and to see the rules of creating a Super Culture™ through the eyes of a true cultural architect.

Chris's insights are not just theories; they are lived experiences that have shaped companies and leaders alike. He has mastered the art of making culture not just a concept, but a daily practice that drives success. We are proud to call him a friend.

- Kelley Babcock and Terri Norvell, Co-Founders,
Leadership Growth Formula

Introduction

Nearly 90% of people hate their job, feel underappreciated, and are frustrated. Too many companies have bad environments full of diminished morale and productivity, and this diminished morale and productivity leads to unachieved goals and even bankruptcy, crushing the hopes and dreams of CEOs and employees.

People are searching for a better way to fix this problem. Only, they're often looking in the wrong direction. CEOs are asking the wrong questions and seeking quick-fix solutions for complex dilemmas.

Often, keynotes don't address the right issues. Partly because most of those aren't given by someone who's been there, failed, and brought happiness into their culture and success to the business. They focus on talking about company core values and mission statements without developing a solid process that aligns the culture with goals and vision. These are good items to develop, but they're not the things that increase production and employee retention.

Understanding how to create a Super Culture™ to develop an environment of greatness is critical to guiding your company and team to success. It can change your life and the lives of those around you. Your business production increases, you hit your goals, and even achieve more than you thought possible. Your team achieves more than they believed possible and feel appreciated for it.

Creating a Super Culture™ is something any entrepreneur, CEO, or employee can help achieve. It is a proven step-by-step process that is simple, fun, engaging, and effective. It adds energy, pride, and wellness into the team. The Super Culture™ process works at home and work, and it is capable of improving multiple aspects of your life.

Within a Super Culture™, people feel invigorated to go to work in the morning. When they walk in the door, they know they will hit their goals for the day and will be appreciated for it. They aren't going to look for work elsewhere in the hopes of finding a better work environment because they love where they work now.

A business that builds the Super Culture™ understands how to retain its best workers and how to train people toward personal success. The company becomes known as one of the best places to work and customers feel valued, which leads to better sales.

You can say your culture is great, but you still aren't hitting your goals. In reality, the two are aligned in a Super Culture™. This book shows you where the gaps are and talks about how to fix them. It's not extraordinarily difficult, and change is not impossible.

You can choose not to give your company, team, and yourself a chance to experience how the Super Culture™ improves everything. You can keep losing your best people to other opportunities. You can feel stressed out about not making your company goals...again.

But you don't have to. Within this book are the 5 simple steps to take your company from a stress-filled environment to one of greatness. You can feel happy to walk in the door and get to work for the day. You can create your goals, feel confident in hitting them, and often achieve more than you thought possible.

I've been where you are, and I created a Super Culture™ that took my company from the brink of bankruptcy. The steps inside this book empowered me to build that same company into a million-dollar company. If you're ready to experience the same journey with your business, let's get started.

Five Simple Rules To Create A Super Culture™

Rule 1: It All Starts With You

Rule 2: Write It Down

Rule 3: Praise What You Want Repeated™

Rule 4: Hold It Accountable

Rule 5: Protect & Thrive

CHAPTER 1

Does Your Work Environment Suck?

"The first step of improvement is becoming aware that a problem exists."

~Chris Cornelison

That One Conversation On The Plane

I was traveling back from a business conference focused on strategic coaching, and as many people do on the plane, I had a conversation with the person next to me. She noticed some of the materials I was reviewing from the conference I attended, and she started asking me questions. We got into an engaging conversation about culture, environment, and business.

When I spoke to her, the thing that really struck me was when we talked about what makes her unhappy about her work culture. She started with, "You know, my boss is an a**hole." This led us down a path of exploring her work days, and it became clear that her work environment just didn't sound great. She was stressed out, worn out, and felt like no one appreciated her.

For the rest of the flight, I took her through the Super Culture™ framework—the same one I will introduce you to inside this book. By the time the plane landed, she told me she felt more confident and in control of her situation. She had a direction to follow that would help her improve her work environment instead of just "dealing with it."

I Hear This All The Time

I travel a lot, giving keynote speeches, training, and mentoring to businesses of all sizes across multiple industries. No matter the size or type of business, I hear the same things over and over.

- People will jump ship and leave our company for as little as a dollar-an-hour pay raise.
- The newest generation in the workforce is lazy, and I can't communicate with them.
- I've had a garbage can moment. (We will get into this later.)
- My Boss is a Jerk
- I am burned out
- There is no clear growth path
- **Most Of All, I hear, "I Feel Unappreciated."**

Statistics show that 52% of people feel unappreciated in the workforce[1], and that becomes the top reason many quit. Money

---

[1] Parker, Kim, and Juliana Menasce Horowitz. "Majority of Workers Who Quit a Job in 2021 Cite Low Pay, No Opportunities for Advancement, Feeling Disrespected." Pew Research Center, 9 Mar. 2022, www.pewresearch.org/short-reads/2022/03/09/majority-of-workers-who-quit-a-job-in-2021-cite-low-pay-no-opportunities-for-advancement-feeling-disrespected/. Accessed 26 June 2024.

usually becomes a distant third or fourth reason for quitting when people are already making enough to pay their bills.

Not only will they possibly quit, but while they are with the company, they will underachieve, pull away from the team, and destroy the culture.

It's the same from the Nuclear Strategic Leadership Conference to the Tax Collector Association, in-house printing, pharmacies, healthcare companies, retails, credit unions, teachers, and coaches—wherever there is a workforce environment, there is a need for Super Culture™. There hasn't been an industry I've given a keynote to or taught a class to that hasn't benefited from the 5 Simple Rules outlined in this book.

"Normal Culture"

In today's workplace, you mostly find what I call Normal Culture. So, the real question is, what do most people think the definition of normal culture is? Several years ago, I searched the internet and came across this definition.

> **The Internet's Definition of Normal Culture:**
>
> "The beliefs and behaviors that determine how a company's employees and management interact with each other and handle outside business transactions. **It's usually based on the personalities and opinions of the employees and management.**"

I don't have a problem with the first sentence of this definition. This is how we show up. This is how we treat each other. This is how we treat the customer. It is the "second sentence" that bothers me when it says, "It's usually based on the personalities and opinions of the employees and management."

In other words, normal culture is not based on the CEO's vision or mission. It is not based on company goals. It is not based on the things that are on your job description or position agreement or even your own personal goals. It is just based on people showing up in basically good or bad moods. That is not culture; that is just what I like to call "temperament."

That makes you a victim to one thing, and one thing ONLY, for the rest of your professional career. And that one thing is simple: do people show up in a good or bad mood?

This leads to several bad things for the employee, the team, and the company.

Let's look at what actually happens in the real world:

- Most employees take a job with every intent of being successful. They come in and honestly try to work hard and usually do a good job in the beginning.

- The boss never tells the employee clearly what they want them to do. Nothing's written down, especially in smaller companies. There is no job description or culture document, so the employee tries to figure it out by seeing what everyone else is doing.

- The employee eventually has a bad interaction with the boss. Maybe they didn't do what the boss expected them to do or didn't do it correctly, or perhaps they had a bad interaction with a customer.

- The employee gets mad and goes into a mental hijack (I'll go over this in Chapter 3).

- In turn, the boss gets mad and also goes into a mental hijack (also in Chapter 3).

- Then, from that point on, your work culture diminishes a little more each day for the life of the business or for that employee until they get frustrated enough to leave.

NORMAL CULTURE

MOST EMPLOYEES THAT START A NEW
JOB WORK HARD AND DESIRE SUCCESS

THE BOSS NEVER TELLS THE EMPLOYEE
CLEARLY WHAT THEY WANT THEM TO DO
(NOTHING IS WRITTEN DOWN)

THE EMPLOYEE EVENTUALLY HAS A BAD
INTERACTION WITH BOSS AND UNDERPERFORMS

THE EMPLOYEE FEELS UNAPPRECIATED OR GETS
MAD AND GOES INTO MENTAL HIJACK

THE BOSS GETS MAD AND GOES
INTO MENTAL HIJACK

CULTURE GOES DOWN
FOREVER

Normal culture is why people feeling underappreciated or sensing a lack of empathy from leadership has become the number one problem in the workforce. It begins with the honeymoon phase, during the first 30-60 days of employment, where everything starts off great, but then things often get stuck. This throws culture out of alignment and puts the employee on a downward trend of mediocracy from that point on. Things spiral into frustration and poor performance until the employee is stuck and burnt out. This book is going to change all of that! (We will explore why this happens and what you can do about it in the hiring, training, and firing sections during Chapter 7).

Normal culture leads your company to...

- High turnover rates.
- Stressed out management and workers.
- Underachievement on all levels.
- No one's hitting their goals (not the individual, not the company).
- Feeling stuck.
- Workplace exhaustion.
- Anxiety and depression.
- Low energy.
- Lack of motivation.

Is this really the culture that you want to work in and what you want your team to work in every day? What if there was a better way to create a better culture in your company? What if you could flip all those things into a work environment that everyone, including yourself, looked forward to every day? **An environment of greatness.**

We're going to get away from the idea that good and bad moods control your everyday. We are going to flip the overwhelming thoughts of "nobody is listening to me," "nobody cares," "the customer doesn't care," and "the employee doesn't care" into an environment of greatness where everyone feels appreciated, the team works together toward clear goals, and has a successful environment.

It is time to break free of the "normal culture." In this book, I will introduce the 5 Simple Rules that create a roadmap out of a toxic workplace environment and into what I call a Super Culture™.

Now that we have explained what Normal Culture looks like, let's look at how a Super Culture™ pulls out all the greatness deep inside you and your team and will CHANGE YOUR LIFE FOREVER!

Key Takeaways

- ✓ **First Step: Recognize the Problem:** You can't fix what you don't know is broken. A lot of people are stuck in work environments that drain the life out of them, and they don't even realize there's a better way.

- ✓ **"Normal Culture" Ain't Working:** Most workplaces are run on what I call "normal culture," where everyone's just reacting to moods, personalities, and confusion about what's expected. It's a fast track to burnout, frustration, and the team feeling underappreciated.

- ✓ **Feeling Unappreciated is Huge:** One thing I hear all the time is, "I don't feel appreciated." That's a way bigger reason people quit than money. If someone doesn't feel valued, they'll either quit or worse— they'll stay and do the bare minimum.

✓ **Super Culture™ is the Way Forward:** The good news is, it doesn't have to stay like this. I'm going to explain the 5 Simple Rules to shift from that "normal culture" to a Super Culture™—where your team feels appreciated, motivated, and excited to show up. Trust me, this is going to change everything for you and your business.

CHAPTER 2

Introducing Super Culture™

"The only competitive advantage you have complete control over is your culture."

~Reid Hoffman, Co-founder of LinkedIn

What Is A Super Culture™?

Super Culture™:

A written-down and protected environment of greatness. It is complete with fun, love, leadership, accountability, and compassion—both for the team and customers!

Super Culture™ is an environment where we can achieve the impossible. It is an environment where we expect to do great things. It is protected by leadership through accountability. You absolutely must have accountability to build an environment of greatness. We are not striving for an environment of average.

The Bottom Line Is

<u>This is how we show up and get things done.</u>

Transforming a Normal Culture Into a Super Culture™

Let's look at the powerful difference a few simple rules can make.

- In a Super Culture™, there are short written documents that clearly tell the team and every member how to do a great job. This creates clarity. (Chapter 4)

- Now the leader knows clearly how to consistently lead and train the team on what to accomplish.

- Employees still work hard, but now they choose a great attitude because they understand the environment and are on the same page with the team.

- The leader now praises the great day-to-day accomplishments with the power of praise. (Chapter 5)

- The employee now feels appreciated, enjoys what they do, takes pride in it, and thrives.

- The leader now feels appreciated, enjoys what they do, takes pride in it, and thrives. (Chapter 7)

- An environment of greatness is created that makes the employee, team, and company thrive forever! (Chapter 7)

SUPER CULTURE

WRITTEN DOCUMENTS SET CLEAR GOALS

⬇

THE LEADER TELLS THE EMPLOYEE CLEARLY WHAT
THEY WANT THEM TO DO

⬇

THE EMPLOYEE WORKS HARD AND CHOOSES
A GREAT ATTITUDE

⬇

THE LEADER PRAISES EFFORTS

⬇

THE EMPLOYEE ENJOYS AND THRIVES

⬇

THE LEADER ENJOYS AND THRIVES

⬇

CULTURE IMPROVES FOREVER

⬇

COMPANY THRIVES

How Super Culture™ Impacts The Company

- The company attracts and retains the best-in-class employees. I like to call them Eagles.
- Team members feel a sense of pride and fulfillment in their work.
- Big goals that no one thought possible are achieved.
- Future leaders are developed and mentored.
- People and the company thrive and win awards.
- The company becomes best in class.
- Everyone is achieving what seemed unachievable and loving it!

Super Culture™ empowers everyone on the team to be a part of achieving greatness, and it creates more revenue than you ever imagined. Once you create a Super Culture™, you will never turn back. You become that top 10% in your industry. People see your success, and they want to be a part of it.

Now...I Know What You Are Thinking

One or more of these thoughts may be going through your head right now:

- Yeah, but wait...This all sounds too good to be true.
- My industry is different.
- This won't work at my company.
- Yes, but we tried that already, and...
- Oh, great. More "Rah, Rah!" motivation.
- It's too hard. There's no way...
- We've been down this culture path before and...

- It won't last, so why bother? It wears off in time.
- I can't change. I am just not built that way.
- My team doesn't want this stuff.

I hear you. I once was you. I've been where you're sitting now, having those same thoughts. In fact, in August of 2000, I was on my knees next to my trash can, inches away from bankruptcy and at my wit's end. My company was trapped in Normal Culture. In order to free myself and everyone else, I had to create a Super Culture™.

My Journey To Creating A Super Culture™

I grew up working in my grandparents' pharmacy from the time I was 12 years old. It was my dream job to come back and own it one day; so naturally, I went to pharmacy school. After graduating from pharmacy school, I went straight back to work at the pharmacy.

My granddad was a great guy, and I felt like my grandparents were a second set of parents to me. They built a really nice small business. My grandad did, however, make a common mistake that a lot of leaders and small business owners make; he never wrote anything down. Everyone in this family business were great people, but no one knew exactly what their role on the team was. We didn't have a vision or mission statement—no goals, no processes, and for sure, no culture document. We didn't even have job descriptions! Your job description was, "work hard," "figure it out," or "do what is supposed to be done." This led to a lot of dissension, bickering, drama, and chaos. There were a lot of people saying things like, "That's not my job," or "Someone else is supposed to do that." And that is where I came into the picture.

I was 24 years old—young, intelligent, very competitive, had a great work ethic, and was fresh out of college. That probably doesn't sound too bad, but let me give the rest of the story. I was a know-it-all with poor leadership skills, slight anger management issues, and zero emotional intelligence! I didn't even know emotional intelligence existed, much less what it was and how to use it. And I was going to step in and save the day. (Yeah…right!)

I am sure you have all worked with the young gun straight out of college who thinks they know everything. Right? To top all this off, my grandparents were aging. About three months after I graduated pharmacy school, my grandparents decided to go into semi-retirement! That meant that they spent the next six months of the year in sunny Florida. And they did this every year for the first three years of my career! We literally had no management structure at all.

Now, don't hear me wrong; I was actually a really good pharmacist at this time in my career. My grandparents taught me to have a great work ethic and how to be compassionate with patients. I was great at filling the prescriptions very fast and accurately. So, I was good at doing my job (or pacesetting leadership, which we will discuss in Chapter 4). But I was destroying the culture! How was I doing a good job AND destroying the culture, you ask? By constantly yelling all day, making everyone uncomfortable, having a bad attitude, and making sure everyone around me knew just how good I was at doing my job (or how much better I was than they were). No one could work as fast and accurately as I could;

no one knew as much as I did or lived up to my expectations. I constantly said things to the team like, "If everyone worked as hard as I do," "If everyone could fill prescriptions as quickly as I do," or "If everyone paid as much attention to details as I do"— BLAH BLAH BLAH! And day in and day out, I created about as bad a work environment as possible.....And then it happened!

The Day I Had Been Waiting for FINALLY CAME!

Three years into my career, my grandparents decided they wanted to retire and sell the store. And guess who decided to buy that store? The arrogant young guy who thought he knew it all.

When my grandparents sold the pharmacy to me, I stepped in and probably did exactly what you thought this immature owner would do. I stepped in and said, "I'm the boss now!" "I'm going to crack the whip," and "I am going to straighten this thing out!" "Everyone is going to do it my way!" And I yelled, and I fussed, and I cussed, and made everybody on my team absolutely miserable.

And then, just 7 months into ownership, I had taken a long-respected family business to the brink of financial failure. I took a pharmacy that was slightly profitable when I bought it, and in seven months, I drove it all the way into the red. I was failing on every level, and all that led me to my garbage can and the day that changed my life forever.

The Day That Changed My Life Forever

Like most days, I arrived an hour before the store opened to try and get ahead. My team arrived on time, an hour later, just like they were supposed to do. Being the great leader I was then, I greeted them with a sarcastic tone and stern look with my motivational start to the day. "I have already filled thirty prescriptions this morning. Surely, now that all of you are here, we can stay caught up!" Not very motivational, right?

Now, I know you may not be familiar with pharmacy. What I just did before anyone else arrived was equivalent to about two hours of work production for two people. So, having a great work ethic and being good at your job will NOT solely create a good culture.

By lunchtime, you probably guessed it…we were behind, and the only way to catch up was for me to skip lunch. Like always, I could not let it go, and I made sure everyone on the team knew of my sacrifice with, "I wish I was getting to go to lunch, but I don't get to go to lunch. I have done more work than anyone else, but I don't get to go to lunch because we are so far behind."

Finally, closing time rolls around, and we're still behind. I was going to have to stay late once again, but it was time for my team to go home. So, in true gentlemanly fashion, I escorted my team to the front of the store and held the door open for them as they passed by me to leave. I had to give them one last bit of motivation for the next day before they left, so I said, "I wish I was getting to go home. I was the first one here. I did more than anyone else, but I have to stay and finish the work because there's still work to be done!"

I let the door to the pharmacy close behind them, and I sent my team home absolutely miserable to their families after they worked their butts off all day long for me. I have no doubt that there were many days I sent them home so miserable they were to the point of tears from the crap environment that they had to work in. I am ashamed of that to this day, but at that time in my life, I didn't know what to do...so I locked myself in the store and returned to work like I had done many times before.

Then, Everything Changed

But this night was different. The stress of our failing finances, how I knew I was making my team miserable, and how I was making myself miserable just erupted.

The tension built as I filled prescriptions as fast as I could well past closing. As the bottles kept covering the counter, I was getting madder and madder and madder. Then it happened! I finally did what all people with 0 emotional intelligence, poor leadership skills, and anger issues are going to do at some point. I slammed my spatula on the countertop. BAM! I threw all those bottles across the pharmacy. I yelled every cuss word I knew, and let me tell you, I knew a lot of cuss words! And I kicked my garbage can so hard it doubled to the floor.

That's right, everything sucked. I sucked. My team sucked. My life sucked. My garbage can even sucked because it was dented all the way to the floor, so it couldn't even hold garbage. I was an inch from bankruptcy, and for the first time in my life, I was failing on every level.

What If It Was Me?

I truly started soul-searching that night because I didn't want this anymore. I started cleaning up the mess caused by the immature leader I was at this time. I picked up all the bottles and put everything back in order, and began popping out the garbage can. It wasn't the first time I kicked that garbage can in, but let me tell you, it would be my last.

As I popped that garbage can out, this question started rolling through my mind, and it just would not go away. It became my epiphany that night.

That question was simply: **What if it was me?**

What if I was the problem? What if everybody around me was working really hard, but I gave them no guidance on what I wanted them to do every day? What if I was a poor leader? I can honestly say I had never been around any great mentor leaders before this time.

What if it was me? I pondered that question for another hour, and the important thing to really take notice of was my WHY. Why that question?

It was "the people" I sent home miserable to their families that night. You see, I truly loved those people. I loved them like my own family, and they were really good people. I hate thinking about how I treated them early in my career, but I did love them.

So, what if it was me? At the end of that hour, I came to the hardest conclusion I had ever reached in my whole career.

IT WAS ME.

I was the problem. I was the common denominator to everything going wrong in the company. It was me. And as hard as that night was to accept, it was the first step of a leadership journey I would be on for the rest of my life. It caused me to create what I call SUPER CULTURE™! And I would like to spend the rest of this book sharing the 5 Simple Rules so you, too, can create your own Super Culture™.

The 5 Simple Rules to Create a Super Culture™

That night, when I realized it all started with me, it changed my life and that of my company. My epiphany transformed a team that needed the guidance and direction that I wasn't giving them into a world-famous Super Culture™. A Super Culture™ that brought my company back from the brink of bankruptcy. It allowed me to build our business into a million-dollar company.

In this book, I will take you through the 5 simple rules that make a Super Culture™.

- **Rule 1**: It all starts with you (just like it did with me). Chapter 3 will show you how understanding leadership and emotional intelligence starts the journey

- **Rule 2:** Write it down, or it does not exist. Chapter 4 will show you the 5 main documents you need to create a Super Culture™.

- **Rule 3**: Praise what you want repeated™. Chapter 5 shows how to use the power of praise to motivate people to show up, work hard, and create maximum focus.

- **Rule 4:** Hold it accountable. Chapter 6 shows how to hold accountability while still honoring the culture and how being accountable plays a critical role in the Super Culture™.

- **Rule 5**: Protect & thrive. In Chapter 7, we will go through how establishing rules for hiring, training, firing, and rewarding plays a part in the Super Culture™.

You may be the owner and ultimate creator of your whole company culture, the leader of your department, or a team member like the lady on the plane. But no matter your position on the team or in your company, you can help create a Super Culture™. Let's begin with *Rule 1: It all starts with you* in the next chapter.

Key Takeaways

✓ **Super Culture™ is the Secret Sauce:** Super Culture™ isn't just about clocking in—it's about creating a written, protected environment of greatness with leadership, fun, love, accountability, and compassion for both the team and customers. It's what takes you from average to extraordinary.

✓ **Clarity Beats Chaos:** Turning a normal culture into a Super Culture™ starts with clear, written expectations. When everyone knows exactly what's expected of them, the whole team thrives and takes pride in their work, and the leader can actually lead.

✓ **Super Culture™ Brings Big Wins:** A Super Culture™ doesn't just make people happier—it helps you attract the best people, hit big goals you never thought possible, and grow future leaders. Everyone thrives, the company succeeds, and the sky's the limit.

✔ **It Starts With You:** Just like I had to face the hard truth that I was the problem, you have to start with yourself. The 5 Simple Rules I'll share in this book are the blueprint to creating your own Super Culture™ and changing everything for the better.

CHAPTER 3

Rule 1 – It All Starts With You

> *"The true leader serves others."*
>
> ~ John C. Maxwell

The Number 1 Thing A Leader Does: Serve Others

All improvement starts with awareness. For the first time in my life, I realized I was the root of all the problems with my company; however, I had no idea what to do next. It was definitely time to take a long, hard look in the mirror and decide who I wanted to be.

The one thing I knew was I did not want to be the jerk kicking the garbage can for the rest of my life. So, I started reading every leadership book I could find. I hired a business coach. I attended keynotes. I joined a business development organization, and I started doing everything I could to improve.

I was HUNGRY for answers.

The first thing I learned is that no matter which leadership guru I studied they all agreed with one major point:

The number one thing a leader does is serve others.

At this point in my career, I wasn't serving ANYONE, but I was more than ready to learn how.

Early on in my career, I didn't get it. When I kicked that garbage can, I wasn't focused on anybody else or how my emotions and actions affected "them." I learned that a leader serves others in several different ways.

You get the honor of serving others through setting goals, coaching, teaching, sharing the "why's," showing patience, providing resources, giving vision, and, most of all, by helping them grow confidence in "themselves." These all lead you to serve others by making sure you, the team, and the company grow at all times.

Everything rises and falls on leadership and accountability (more on this coming in Chapter 6).

Emotional Intelligence
The Biggest Competitive Advantage In The World

It didn't take me long in my leadership journey to stumble onto what I believe is the biggest competitive advantage in the world—and that is Emotional Intelligence. To be able to serve others, you must understand how emotions affect you <u>and</u> your team.

I've used emotional intelligence to negotiate, coach teams, grow my organizations, and be a better person, business owner, CEO, leader, parent, friend, and husband. I believe it's the biggest competitive advantage that exists in the world, and I believe that less than 10% of the people in the world across all industries actually understand and use what I'm about to teach you in the next few pages.

Dr. Eric Thomas says "that the inability to self-assess is why most people fail." I had to ask myself, *what makes people not self-assess?* It's because they don't understand emotional intelligence and the brain. They get stuck in a negative cycle and make the same mistakes using the same bad habits over and over…in some cases forever!

So, I'm going to give you the simplest and most usable neuroscience lesson in the world over the next few pages. Read it slowly or read it a few times—whatever it takes for you to absorb the rest of this chapter. You master this, and it will change your life, because **Rule #1 of creating a Super Culture™ is it all starts with you**! When you understand emotional intelligence, you will always have a way to stop, self-assess, and make a controlled decision on how to improve.

Emotional intelligence has three phases:

Three Phases of Emotional Intelligence

Phase 1: Emotional Awareness
Phase 2: Emotional Control
Phase 3: Emotional Improvement

Every phase involves how emotions affect you and others around you. First, remember **Rule 1: It all starts with you.** Do not try to fix others first; make progress on your own personal habits and your own awareness. Then, you can help others.

The summaries of each phase of emotional intelligence are below. I'll do my best to describe each one in detail for you.

EMOTIONAL INTELLIGENCE

Phase 1 EMOTIONAL AWARENESS
The ability to identify your own emotions and those of others.

Phase 2 EMOTIONAL CONTROL
The ability to harness emotions and apply them to tasks like thinking and problem-solving.

Phase 3 EMOTIONAL IMPROVEMENT
The ability to regulate your own emotions, and the ability to cheer up or calm down another person and spark work improvement.

©Cornelison2023

Phase 1: Emotional Awareness

Emotional awareness is the ability to identify your own emotions and those of others around you. This is literally the ability to be aware that the situation is making you feel something. The situation could be making me or my team mad, fearful, stressed out, embarrassed, etc.

First, you have to identify your emotions. You acknowledge how the current situation or event affects you emotionally. Then, you can become aware of the exact same types of emotions and how they are affecting others around you.

In other words, you begin to see how a situation affects your actions first, and then how your emotions and actions make others around you uncomfortable.

Most people in most companies never become aware of their own emotional reactions to their problems. Therefore, most people never leave phase one. This is because of the **amygdala hijack**. If you never gain awareness of your emotions, you stay stuck reacting the same way to the same problems your whole life. It all starts with you gaining control of your emotions so you can maintain the ability to think and problem solve and improve the current situation, which is Phase 2. Then, Phases 2 and 3 allow you to start understanding when the emotions of your employees, team members, and colleagues are shutting them down.

> An amygdala hijack is a fight-or-flight response. The amygdala section of your brain defines and regulates emotions and activates the fight-or-flight response.

Let me give you a real-life example.

When my son went to college, I had some trouble having conversations with him. Every day, I tried to use my knowledge of emotional intelligence and have good conversations with him. Every day, I immediately shut him down, and we ended up arguing. Once someone shuts down, you just have to stop. There is nothing going forward because they are now mad and are in an amygdala hijack. They literally don't hear or comprehend anything you tell them next no matter how helpful it seems to you. Therefore, we had the same argument over and over and over…day after day after day.

Then, it suddenly hit me one day. I used one word every time I spoke with him, and that one word was tripping his amygdala. That word was "immature;" he was 19 years old and didn't want to be called immature, which is how I was actually starting every conversation.

Whenever I used the word immature—BOOM!—he shut down. The minute I was aware of that, I removed the word immature from our conversations. We started having good conversations from that time onward.

It starts with YOUR awareness first, then, you help them with THEIR awareness.

I used this emotional awareness tactic to fix the communication issue with my son without drawing attention to it. I just removed the word from our conversations, and he stopped shutting down. Anytime you can identify a trigger causing you or others to shut down, you can start trying to remove it. Then and only then can you move on to Phase 2.

Phase 2: Emotional Control

Emotional control means harnessing emotions and applying them to tasks such as "thinking and problem-solving." This is very important because if you can't control your emotions, you cannot think and problem-solve. You just get mad, and react over and over in the exact same way…sometimes forever!

For example, my company gets busy, I get mad, I yell at the team, the team shuts down, my company loses efficiency, the garbage can gets kicked in, and then, it **repeats**. With emotional control, you become aware that your reaction to the problem is not helping, and you seek out a new choice.

I would have been kicking that garbage can all the way to bankruptcy if I hadn't stepped back and gotten some awareness. It requires thinking and problem-solving—both of which you cannot do if you don't understand emotional intelligence and the brain. When you cannot think, you cannot reach Phase Two, and if you have no "emotional control," you cannot think. This is why most people spend their entire lives without ever getting any real control over actions that keep them away from improving and keep them from the greatness they have inside of themselves.

Phase 3: Emotional Improvement

This is upper-level stuff. Don't try to start with phase three. Phase three is the ability to regulate and use your own emotions, to cheer up or calm down another person, and in the end spark work improvement.

This is why companies around the country turn to me to help them; it is the ability to spark work improvement they are after. When you become efficient at understanding emotional intelligence, you can start to notice when people are shutting down, know when to push, and know when not to. You can coach them to become aware of themselves and identify the situation causing the problem.

Again, this is upper-level stuff. Do not start here. It all starts with you. If we become aware and quit shutting down our brains, we can find the solution and improve. We can improve ourselves, our team, and our environment and thus improve everything else.

Next, we'll discuss the three things happening in the brain so you can fully utilize emotional intelligence. Understand this, and you'll be on your way to improving your leadership and creating your own Super Culture™.

The Brain—Amygdala Hijack—and Emotional Intelligence

You may not be completely bought in yet, but let me explain a little more about the brain, and you will understand it all.

If I tell you that our hearts beat the same way, you get it. Your heart may be stronger than mine, but both our hearts work and beat the same way. If I tell you our lungs work the same way, you get it. Your lungs may be stronger than mine, but we all breathe in oxygen, and we breathe out carbon dioxide. Therefore, they work the same way.

Our brains operate on the same principle. Your brain and mine use the same pathways and mechanisms to function. Don't get me wrong here. Everyone reading this book has unique life experiences, beliefs, backgrounds, and core values that make you all unique human beings, but the pathways of the brain still function the same way.

Our brains work the same based on what happens to us and the emotions surrounding those experiences. So, let's take a look at exactly how the brain reacts.

The Three Parts Of The Brain

When you understand these three parts of the brain, you understand the three phases of emotional intelligence much better.

- The Subconscious Brain
- The Conscious Brain
- The Amygdala

The Subconscious Brain

Let's start with our subconscious brain. Our subconscious brain houses 90-95% of all thoughts and actions. **This phase is 80 times faster than the conscious brain,** which gives humans the remarkable ability to do work tasks really fast. You probably had a coach tell you, "Don't think, just react." Good reactions or subconscious habits can be very, very positive. They can help you create a very efficient skillset. So, as long as your subconscious habits are good, you're crazy efficient. Bad reactions, however, can be very bad and leave you suffering from negative results forever if you can't become aware.

Let me give you a simple example of brushing your teeth. When you brush your teeth, you put no conscious thought into it. You don't say: let me take off the top of the toothpaste, let me grab the toothpaste and squeeze it gently to produce a pea-sized amount of toothpaste onto the brush, then tilt the brush at a 45-degree angle and make circular contact with the teeth, and so on. No, you just brush your teeth completely subconsciously. You can probably brush your teeth, yell at the kids, listen to a song, and scan social media at the same time….all subconsciously.

Another example is, you don't think about how to drive to work. You do all the actions of starting the car, pulling into traffic, and navigating traffic without thinking, without using your conscious brain, because we are in our subconscious brain 90% of the day. Hence, you are continuously making thousands of little quick subconscious decisions, good or bad, with no real thought.

The Conscious Brain

We are actually only in conscious thinking for about 5-10% of the day. In other words, only 5-10% of our daily thoughts and actions are actually conscious thoughts. However, these conscious thoughts "**allow us the ability to change**." The conscious part of the brain is the part that actually makes us human beings. It's the brain's prefrontal cortex, and we have the largest one of any mammal. Without that large prefrontal cortex, we would be much more like a dog, a deer, a lizard, etc. We would react to situations, but we wouldn't be able to think of ways to improve our situation. So, we have to be in conscious thinking to create awareness and be able to think of a better solution to a problem.

If you cannot get into conscious thinking, you cannot enter Phase 2 of emotional intelligence that we just talked about. You lose the human ability to think and problem-solve. You become stuck doing the same thing over and over again with the same energy-draining effects of having a normal culture. People get worn down by the same daily problems and end up hating their jobs. People will leave your company for as little as a dollar and hour pay raise just to move into another bad culture.

Amygdala Hijack

The final part of the brain you need to understand is the amygdala. It is literally meant to answer the question "Do I eat it, or does it eat me?" and prepare us to fight or flight.

The amygdala is a tiny walnut-sized part of the brain, but it's also very powerful. What I need you to understand is when the amygdala fires, it wins. It immediately shuts down your conscious thinking and goes directly into subconscious habits whether or not they are good or bad.

Fight Or Flight Mode

Let's go back to the caveman days when we were faced with a lot of life-and-death situations. Let's say I'm a caveman, and my family hasn't eaten for four days. I've got to kill something and drag it home, or my family is going to starve. So, I craft a wooden spear and hide in a tree, hoping something comes under it. A wild boar comes under, and I look at that wild boar and I think this would feed my family, but this might also kill me. I'm weak.

I only have a wooden spear, and I have to make a decision right now–it's life or death!

If I decide to fight, my amygdala will be triggered. When the amygdala triggers, we immediately go into subconscious thinking. Your brain triggers your body for fight or flight by shutting down your conscious brain and using all your hormones and neurotransmitters to fuel your body for the best chance to survive. In this case, it's fight, so I'll jump out of that tree, kill the wild boar, and drag that meat home for my family.

Now, the opposite caveman scenario may be to imagine I'm on the hunt, walking through the jungle, and a saber-toothed tiger jumps out. I don't need my conscious brain to say, "Hmmm... there's a very large tiger. He's running at me. He may attack and kill me." No! I need my amygdala to trip and my subconscious brain to kick in, and fuel me to run! I'm in flight mode.

> **This is the main point you need to understand.**
>
> We cannot be in amygdala hijack and conscious thinking at the same time. When the amygdala fires, we lose the ability to think and problem-solve because our conscious brain is shut down and we go directly to subconscious habits. No matter how silly or bad those habits are, like yelling, cussing, or even kicking in a garbage can.

We cannot be in amygdala hijack and conscious thinking at the same time. Our brains don't work like that. If you cannot control your emotions enough to not fire your amygdala, you're always going to go into the same subconscious thoughts, and be stuck making the same mistakes over and over again (think back to my story of that last time I kicked the garbage can).

Can you think of anything going on in your own life that may be causing you to react in a way that may be causing you to shut down rather than solve a key problem? I'd encourage you to jot down three things at work that made you angry, fearful, or stressed in the past month. Use this page to make it easy.

WHAT HAPPENS IN AMYGDALA HIJACK

1. THERE IS NO RATIONAL THOUGHT/IT HAPPENS VERY FAST.

2. YOU CAN NOT MAKE SOMEONE COME OUT OF IT; THEY WILL NOT COME OUT OF IT UNTIL THEY "THINK IT'S OVER".

3. OFTEN, PEOPLE WILL BE EMBARRASSED ABOUT HOW THEY ACTED (AND WILL APOLOGIZE).

4. THEY NEED TIME TO REGAIN COMPOSURE.

4 Phases of Amygdala Hijack

1. There are no rational thoughts. The fight or flight response automatically happens and it happens really fast.
2. You can not make someone come out of an amygdala hijack. They will not come out of it until they perceive the threat to be gone. In other words, they will not come out of it until **they believe** it is over.
3. Often, people will be embarrassed about how they acted, and will actually apologize.

4. They need time to regain composure. It takes a lot out of the body to constantly be ready to fight or flight.

Amygdala hijack often happens when two people get into an argument and say those mean, nasty things about one another that they regret later.

The chemical acetylcholine needs to be circulating in the brain for good, clear thought. When the brain goes into hijack it prepares for fight or flight. It takes all the acetylcholine out of the brain and rushes it to other parts of the body. Your shoulders tense up, you get stressed out, and you stay tense (this will be really important in Chapter 5 where you'll learn more about acetylcholine and using praise).

The Snake Story

I usually tell this story at my keynote presentations, as an example of someone experiencing amygdala hijack. Many people fear snakes, right? So, I typically ask for a volunteer out of the audience who has a fear of snakes to help me.

Try to picture a guy (we can call him Hugh) who's really afraid of snakes, volunteering to help me. I'm on stage and say, "Let's pretend I'm a crazy, redneck snake wrangler from Mississippi and I've got snakes in this bag."

I pull out an imaginary bag of snakes and say, "Look, they're moving around. They're the real deal. They're poisonous. They're real snakes and they have real venom."

Hugh starts to picture venomous rattlesnakes in the bag. I walk toward Hugh as I make the motions of untying that imaginary bag of snakes. As it usually happens, Hugh leans back as I approach him. Then, I undo the top of the bag and throw the snakes down in front of Hugh. I tell Hugh to picture an imaginary snake right in front of him coiled to strike at him.

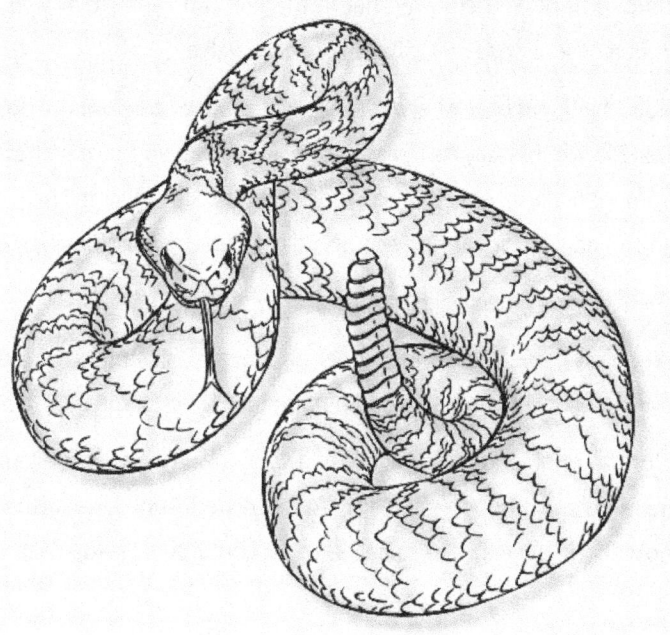

Now, I didn't tell Hugh before, but Aunt Jane had walked up beside him a moment ago. She's in her 90s and moving carefully with her walker. Aunt Jane walked up to Hugh's right shoulder to tell him how he did such a wonderful job on that latest project. Hugh didn't see her walk up because he was focused on the snakes. Those snakes had Hugh's full attention in front of him, and one was coiled right at him.

Hugh doesn't need his conscious brain right now to say, "Hmm.. this crazy man from Mississippi has dumped rattlesnakes in front of me." No, his amygdala is going to fire. What is Hugh going to do next (I ask my volunteer this question)?

Obviously, Hugh is going to jump back really fast. Hugh may yell something defending himself, such as, "What the *bleep* are you doing, you crazy fool!"

At this point, I tell Hugh, "You knocked Aunt Jane over when you jumped back. You elbowed her in the face, and she's bleeding from a busted nose now. She fell over her walker."

Now, the threat hasn't been removed yet, so what would Hugh do next? Hugh may say he'll try to cover Aunt Jane and protect her from more harm, or he may go the other way. Hugh will still be in an amygdala hijack and all actions will still be subconscious

Then I'll ask, "When will Hugh regain his composure?"

When all those snakes are gone, of course. I illustrate this by picking up all those snakes and putting them back in the bag.

I turn to Hugh and the audience and say, "Now, Hugh, you called me a *bleep*, *bleep*, *bleep*. You punched Aunt Jane in the nose, and now we have to call 9-1-1. It could be a life-or-death situation for her.

What will Hugh do next? He will probably apologize for his actions.

Then, what is the last thing Hugh will do? When he finally gets away from all this and goes back to the hotel room, he will need a little time to take a deep breath and try to regain composure.

Hugh has just gone through all the stages of the amygdala hijack.

How Our Brains Have Evolved

Back in the caveman days, we were faced with many life-and-death situations. However, today, we are not. If we get hungry, we go to the grocery store. If we get cold or need shelter, we go inside and turn on the central air/heat. We're just not faced with as many daily life-or-death situations as in the caveman days.

However, our brains have evolved! Due to the Industrial Revolution, technology advances, cell phones, and the internet; we have to make about 10,000 or more daily decisions than they did back in the caveman days.[2] Our amygdala has evolved in a way that it is now triggered by many more things that aren't necessarily life-or-death situations.

Amygdala Hijack In Today's World

Like I said before, our brains have evolved, and different things trigger these hijacks now. It has been scientifically proven by hooking electrodes to the brain that things like fear trigger amygdala hijack. Not life or death fear, but fear of workplace situations. Also, anger, stress, anxiety, drama, embarrassment, and underappreciation have all been scientifically proven to fire the amygdala of our brain in the workplace. This literally means that all of these emotions can eliminate your team's ability to think and problem-solve.[3]

Let's look at some things that may trigger the brain inside your work environment.

---

[2] Krockow, Eva M. "How Many Decisions Do We Make Each Day?" *Psychology Today*, September 2018, www.psychologytoday.com/us/blog/stretching-theory/201809/how-many-decisions-do-we-make-each-day.

[3] Ressler, Kerry J. "Amygdala Activity, Fear, and Anxiety: Modulation by Stress." *Biological Psychiatry*, vol. 67, no. 12, 15 June 2010, pp. 1117–1119, www.ncbi.nlm.nih.gov/pmc/articles/PMC2882379/, https://doi.org/10.1016/j.biopsych.2010.04.027.

- **Fear** of missing the deadline
- **Anger** at the boss who keeps yelling at you in a tone or talking in a manner you don't appreciate
- **Stress** when our equipment went down, or from another angry customer
- **Anxiety** knowing today is going to be really busy, or this project is really hard, or this team we are playing is really good
- **Drama** due to workplace gossip
- **Embarrassment** when people keep calling me names like Gen Z, or Millennial, or lazy, or when people are yelling at me
- **Underappreciation**: Feeling underappreciated is the number one reason people leave their jobs. It's the reason people will leave a job for as little as a dollar-an-hour increase in pay.[4] It can fire the amygdala of your team right when they walk in the door to your facility, if "they believe" that they are not appreciated.

Everyone suffers when their work environment becomes the thing that trips the amygdala as soon as they walk in the front door. The same boss who's yelled at them for years may be there. The tone or sound of the voice may be the trigger. You have to remove the trigger to keep from tripping their amygdala. This can be by awareness of the boss that his/her tone is causing this perception, along with other habits that may be doing the same thing. It could also mean letting the boss go at some point (more on this in Chapter 7).

---

[4] Lipman, Victor. "66% of Employees Would Quit If They Feel Unappreciated." *Forbes*, 15 Apr. 2017, www.forbes.com/sites/victorlipman/2017/04/15/66-of-employees-would-quit-if-they-feel-unappreciated/.

Amygdala Hangover

I came across a term several years ago called "amygdala hangover." This basically means when the amygdala is fired over and over day after day; it takes longer and longer to regain composure and can last up to 4 hours before a team member fully gets back to conscious thinking.

Remember, you can't get out of Phase One of emotional intelligence when you're in an amygdala hijack and therefore cannot think. That means you cannot hear your boss giving you the knowledge you need to fix a problem, you have no emotional awareness and are shut down from receiving whatever they are saying.

As the leader, the first thing you have to do is keep yourself out of amygdala hijack. The next thing you must do is realize when others around you are in it and what caused them to enter the hijack. Your team cannot become aware and improve if you cause them to be in an amygdala hijack all day.

At the beginning of my career, my team would come in, and I would yell at them as they walked in the door. I threw them in the middle of a hijack because they got that every day, and it shut them down for up to four hours. Then, they would go to lunch, and I would yell at them when they returned, putting them right back into the amygdala hijack. I lost my employees for the whole day. There are definitely other ways a leader has to serve others, but it all starts with understanding emotional intelligence.

Super Culture™ Rule #1: It all starts with you.

It all started with me, just like it all starts with you. You must understand leadership and emotional intelligence to create a Super Culture™. We will look at other ways to lead in every chapter.

What are the five leadership styles and how do you use them? How does each style tie into the different levels of your company? Can using the wrong leadership style at the wrong time trigger an amygdala attack? You're ready for the next chapter where I'll answer those questions and more.

Key Takeaways

✔ **Leadership is All About Serving Others:** The number one job of a leader is to serve others. That means guiding your team by setting goals, teaching, showing patience, and helping them build confidence. If you're not serving your people, you're not leading them.

✔ **Emotional Intelligence is Your Secret Weapon:** Emotional intelligence is the biggest competitive edge you can have. It's about understanding your emotions, controlling them, and using them to make better decisions. Master this, and you'll become a better leader, boss, parent, and person.

✔ **The Three Phases of Emotional Intelligence:** First, use awareness of your emotions and how they affect you and your team. Second, control those emotions so you can think clearly and solve problems. Third, use those emotions to improve yourself and your team.

✔ **Amygdala Hijack Will Shut You Down:** When the fight-or-flight response kicks in, your ability to think goes out the window. If you or your team are constantly triggered, you'll just keep repeating the same mistakes. Learn to spot and manage those triggers so you can stay in control.

✓ **It All Starts With You:** If you want to create a Super Culture™, you've got to start with yourself. Understand your own leadership style and get a handle on emotional intelligence. It is the first step to creating a work environment where everyone can thrive.

CHAPTER 4

Rule 2 – Write It Down

"Clear is kind."

~Terri Norvell

Write It Down (or It Does Not Exist).

Now, a lot of people do NOT like Rule Number 2. They tell me things like, "Chris, man, do I really have to write it down? Can't I just show people? Can't I just tell people? Can't they just figure it out?"

If you do not want to write anything down—stop right now. Close the book, go back to normal culture, and know you'll be held hostage for the rest of your career to good or bad moods, and there will be no consistency.

- Writing things down gives the team CLARITY. Remember, "clear is kind."
- Writing things down gives management something to protect.
- Writing things down gives the whole team consistent vocabulary and terminology to use. It gives the coaching

style leadership, discussed later in this chapter, the wording or vocabulary to use when giving the "whys."

There are five documents that I believe are necessary to create a Super Culture™. We will look at each one in this chapter. In my Super Culture™ courses, we have a trademarked process called The 2 Minute Drill™ to help you write these really fast. Also, in my Super Culture™ and leadership classes we give you the templates to address everything each document needs, and training processes to help you build each one of these documents. You can also get instructions and free templates to help you write your own absolutely free at www.chriscornelison.com. You can use the QR code at the end of this book to check them out.

Culture Document

Let's start with the culture document. It is the most important document, and it is the one that is most often left out by companies. Whether it's a large or small business, an athletic team, or a non-profit, it doesn't matter.

With as few as four to five lines, you can totally change the course of your company and create an environment of greatness. Yet, all organizations, in general, make a crucial mistake in failing to take this document seriously.

Many "gurus" will say that core values are enough, but I strongly disagree. I'm passionate that the core values of a company are great to let your people know who you are, but you need the culture document to clearly define the environment of greatness you want inside your company.

> The culture document defines the environment of greatness we are trying to achieve.

Every culture document is unique. I want to share with you my first-ever Super Culture™ document and how it changed my life!

```
IUKA DISCOUNT DRUGS CULTURE
1. BE HAPPY AND HAVE FUN AT WORK
2. YOU CHOOSE YOUR ATTITUDE
3. BE ACCOUNTABLE TO:
    • THE POLICY AND PROCEDURE MANUAL
    • YOUR POSITION AGREEMENT
    • THE COMPANY GOALS
    • THE CULTURE DOCUMENT
4. MAINTAIN A TEAM ENVIRONMENT AT ALL TIMES
```

Let's look at the power of what writing those four lines down did for my company. When you write it down, you create a very important vocabulary that everyone uses and clearly understands, and you give management and leadership something that they can hold accountable.

Line #1: Be Happy And Have Fun At Work.

The reason I wrote this one as my first line was because, at that time in my life, I was miserable! And I had also made everyone around me miserable. My garbage can moment made me realize that I would spend more time at work than I would with my own family for the rest of my life. And the people on my team would spend more time at work than with their own families for the rest of their lives. I owed it to myself and my team to create an environment that we could actually enjoy and not have to be miserable the whole time we were at work.

People tell me all the time, "Chris, you can't hold people accountable to being happy and having fun at work." Let me tell you, you can when you write it down.

We all know what it looks like when somebody isn't happy. When management holds it accountable for you to be happy and have a good time and tries to give you an environment to do it in, you can hold that accountable. This is number one on every culture document for every organization I own. Life is too short to work in an environment you hate. This doesn't mean we should be too quick to fire people, but it does mean we should be willing to let someone go, even if they are good at the skill set of their job, if they are pulling the rest of the team and our culture down.

Line #2: You Choose Your Attitude

I believe most cultures need this one because I can't choose your attitude, and you can't choose mine. I can't make you happy at work, but I can tell you that this is the environment we will have. I'm going to challenge you to choose the concept of Be Happy and Have Fun, but you have to make the ultimate decision to be a part of it and do your own part.

Line #3: Be Accountable To

- The policy and procedure manual
- Your position agreement
- The company goals
- The culture document

I think accountability is a must to have a Super Culture™, and all culture documents need the "be accountable to" statement. Your statement will be different from mine and unique to your company, but it has to be in there.

A Super Culture™ is an environment of greatness where we hit our goals, create new solutions, and conquer things people don't believe are possible. You can be happy and have fun at work on social media, like Facebook or Instagram, playing games, taking a nap, etc. That is NOT a Super Culture™—that is a normal culture. A Super Culture™ holds everyone accountable to the great things we're trying to accomplish as a company.

Now, do not just write down the four things I did. You have to have a policy and procedure manual, a position agreement, and set company goals to hold people accountable to them. YOU have to honor your own culture document first. Have I mentioned how IT ALL STARTS WITH YOU?

Line #4: Maintain A Team Environment At All Times

At the time I built our Super Culture™, we had multiple locations. It was important for us to understand what other people were doing for the good of the company as a whole.

THIS IS A LIVING DOCUMENT

People often avoid writing their culture documents down because they're afraid they'll write the wrong thing. The culture document is a living, breathing document. It can and *should* be changed in the future. This is not the culture document of my company today, but it was my first one and it did change my life. You can see our 2024 Culture Document below, and I make adjustments to it all the time. Also, different corporations, athletic teams, and nonprofits will definitely have different things that are needed to make their environment great. These first four simple lines changed my failing little pharmacy into a multiple-location, multiple-time national award-winning healthcare destination, and they were even highlighted by another author Patti Mara in the book *Up-Solutions* because of the dramatic turnaround we experienced.

This is my current culture document for my supplement company Solutions Rx:

SOLUTIONSRX SUPER CULTURE™ 2024

SolutionsRx

1. HAVE FUN AND BE HAPPY AT WORK!
2. YOU CHOOSE YOUR ATTITUDE
3. BE ACCOUNTABLE TO:
   - THE POLICY AND PROCEDURE MANUAL
   - YOUR POSITION AGREEMENT
   - THE COMPANY GOALS
   - THE CULTURE DOCUMENT
4. BE PRESENT (KNOW WHAT THE COMPANY NEEDS YOU TO DO)
5. WE ARE GRATEFUL AND JOYFUL
6. BE THE BEST
7. WE ADAPT TO CHANGE IN OUR INDUSTRY
8. WE BELIEVE GOOD IS THE ENEMY OF GREAT
9. WE GET THE LITTLE THINGS EXACTLY RIGHT
10. WE HAVE RADICAL HONESTY, TRUTH, AND VULNERABILITY
11. WE LEARN FROM FAILURE FAST AND WE DON'T REPEAT IT
12. WE THINK MODERN AND WE THINK BIG
13. WE SHOW UP ON TIME EVERYWHERE WE ARE SUPPOSED TO BE
14. WE ARE WILLING TO DO WHATEVER IT TAKES FOR HOWEVER LONG IT TAKES TO MEET OUR STANDARDS

We give the culture document to everybody in our company. When we hire new members, we give them this document along with their position agreement. They get both together so we can make sure they have the ability to do the tasks required of them and that they are a good fit for our environment. People will not leave a Super Culture™ for a dollar-an-hour raise. This environment will become one they love and wouldn't dream of leaving. It keeps them growing and supports their family and values financially, spiritually, and mentally. It also instills pride in who they are and what they are accomplishing.

Company Standards

Whereas the culture document is the environment of greatness that we're trying to achieve, the company standards are the minimum we will accept. The company standards outline things like the state and federal laws by OSHA we have to abide by, general cleanliness statements and rules, any tests (such as drug tests) employees have to abide by, and items like these. These are things that you could get fired for or released that day for. I only bring it up as the second document because the two go hand in hand. The Super Culture™ Document is the environment of greatness we want to create and protect, and the Company Standards are the minimum we will accept.

One-Year Vision And Goals

Maybe the most important document for the company is the one-year vision. This document is very important. Special shout out to my long-time business coach and personal friend Paul Simpson for training me so well in how to create them. Paul trained me to have at least a 5-year vision written down, so I believe it's best to have a 1-year and a 5-year vision. This could be one or two documents if you follow my advice and think further out than just the one year, but I've seen a lot of companies experience great success with just having a clear one-year vision to pull goals from.

The whole vision should be a one- to two-page document. The vision shows the team the direction the company needs to go. I use my trademark process, 2 Minute Drill™, to train teams how to write a vision quickly in my 2-day Super Culture™ Class.

I teach entrepreneurs, CEOs, and managers how to pull quarterly goals from the Vision document. This gives trackable and measurable things that drive people toward the vision we are trying to create for the year. It shows how things like profitability, wins, and accountability lead to awards, success, and greatness.

This vision does one more *very* powerful thing for CEOs, entrepreneurs, and leaders. When new deals, products, opportunities, learning opportunities, or new talent to hire come along, it gives you a way to make better decisions. No matter what comes along, you simply ask yourself: is this on vision or off vision? This clarity keeps your company on track to achieve the greatness you set out for without wasting time and resources on the wrong things.

5 Styles of Leadership

Before we look at the organizational structure, I think it is very important for me to give you the 5 styles of leadership you need to master for a Super Culture™. The organizational structure will give you an idea of where and when to use them.

The Five Styles Of Leadership

Importance Of Leadership Styles

Using the wrong style at the wrong time throws Millennials, Gen Z, or any generation into amygdala hijack. It all starts with you. You must understand emotional intelligence and what triggers their amygdala and then serve the team by assisting them in becoming aware. You have to help them harness emotions to think of a solution to the problem and then implement that solution to create a better result.

Visionary Leadership

The Visionary Leader sets the goals, shows clear direction, and provides resources for success. Visionary leadership shows the team where we want to go and how we get there.

Positional Leadership

In my opinion, this is the weakest style of leadership that a leader can use. People only follow positional leadership because they have to. "I am the boss." The positional leader often has the final say. You may be the owner, CEO, manager, head coach, principal, superintendent, whatever. You have a position over others, and just telling them to do something without telling them "why" can really hurt your culture.

Command And Control Leadership

Command and control leadership is relevant in time-sensitive and life-or-death situations. You use forceful motions, orders, yelling, and position to get things done.

Too often, people think back to a high school or college coach yelling at the players and think that's coaching leadership. That is not. It is a command and control style of leadership. You can get away with it sometimes in a coaching, athletic, or military situation because there is a clock and a time-sensitive situation or you are training for life and death situations.

There are very few times in the workforce to use command and control leadership. If you use it at the wrong time and in the wrong situation, it throws your team member into an amygdala hijack. It could shut everybody down, totally inhibiting the awareness of the leader and the team. This eventually leads to the team member feeling unappreciated.

Coaching Style Leadership

This is where you positively influence and teach someone to improve their technique. When you're helping somebody, you show them how to do it. You show them the techniques to get better at it, and you help them improve.

The coaching style invests time and energy into coaching the individual members to improve in the areas your team needs. You help individuals understand their role and coach your team to hit the goals. Unlike the positional leader who never tells the "whys," the coaching style leader always gives the "why" they're doing it that way and how doing things that way benefits the team. Coaching Style Leadership helps each team member and employee understand their role on the team and in the company.

Great managers, coaches, leaders, CEOs, etc. are usually very good with the coaching style of leadership.

50-70% of the leadership you'll use in a Super Culture™ will be the coaching style.

Pace Setting Leadership

You uphold the standards and expectations through pace and production. On an athletic team, the players make the plays, while on a production line, it is the people who do the work. If you're at the customer service level in your organization, you may look at how fast you wait on the customers and what attitude you have with them as the pace-setting part of leadership that we need. Pace-setting leadership is often the style seen by the customer. It is very important to an organization to have great pace-setting leadership.

A Super Culture™ has to be nurtured and protected by leadership. It is really hard to have a team of high-achieving people without anything written down for consistency. It is impossible the bigger your company gets.

The Organizational Chart

Now, the next document I strongly think you need is the organizational chart. Your organizational chart shows what jobs are needed in the company. I think the organizational chart is one of the most "underused" tools by all sizes of companies, especially multi-location and companies with over 100 employees. It tells upper-level management where to go in the company to find the problems that exist. To understand the organizational chart, you MUST understand that different types of leadership exist and when to use them.

The higher up the organization's structure you go, the more visionary leadership you use. The further down you go, the more pace-setting leadership you use. And on each level, as you go up, you use a little more coaching leadership than the level before because you're responsible for the team's performance now.

Notice on the chart below that I don't have command and control or positional leadership listed. This is because those should be used very, very wisely, and very, very rarely. The organizational structure itself gives positional leadership as it usually defines who has the final say in a decision and who is the positional leader, often called the "boss."

The higher you go up on the chart, from a management level to a C- level, the more coaching style leadership you will use. A very common mistake is to promote someone from a tech level because they show great pacesetting leadership and do their particular job really well, but then don't explain to them that the management level requires that they have to transition to using more coaching style leadership to coach the people under them to meet the tasks and hit goals as a team. One way a manager would do this is to teach other people how to be good at the pacesetting aspects of their job. The common mistake a manager makes is to do it themselves, which sets the team up for long-term failure.

Also, the higher up the organizational chart you go, the more visionary leadership you will use. This is usually the owner, entrepreneur, CEO, head coach, superintendent, or whoever is at the C-level or the top. You will direct the team and have to coach people on how to see the company vision clearly. You'll use some visionary leadership all the way down to the front level of the organization because you have to have a vision to see what your role is toward the goals, expectations, and execution the team needs for success for the quarter. You have to be able to say, "Okay, I see how I meet the company vision at the management level or the tech level."

The Tech level is where the goals are hit, the customers are served, and the plays are made. This is the MOST important level of the organizational structure because it is the level that most often interacts with the most important people in the organizational structure, which are the CUSTOMERS! This level uses pacesetting leadership to make sure the customer is served, and the goals are met.

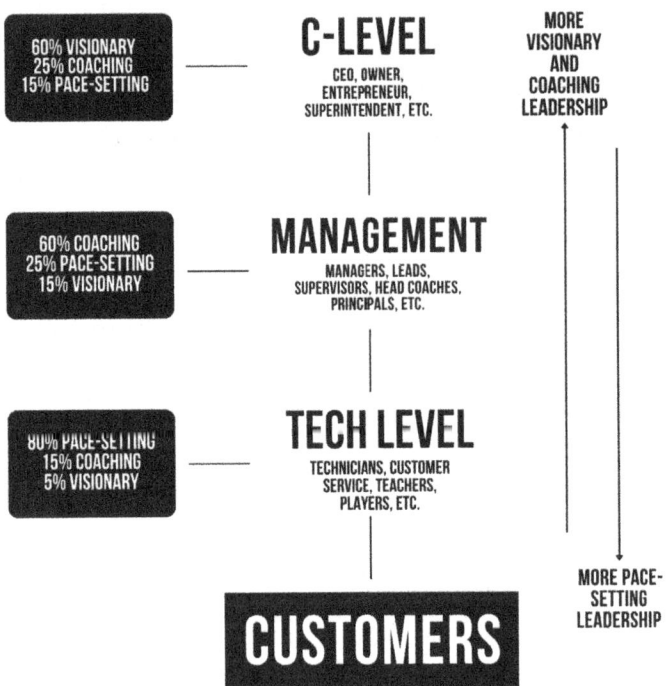

Troubleshooting With The Chart

I have done several on-site visits to companies over the years and leaders will tell me the major problems they have. I can immediately pinpoint where the company needs attention if they have an organizational chart. If sales are low, the problem is usually between the management and tech level. It could be a product problem, a pitch problem, a tech problem, or a management problem, but the organizational structure tells you where to look.

You can highlight the area needing work with a few quick questions and the organizational chart. Then, you can attack the problem with real solutions. The C-level usually needs to understand and use the organizational structure the best.

Position Agreements

Once you have the organizational structure, you need the last document, which is a positional agreement to go with every position you put on the organizational chart. I prefer to use the term position agreements instead of job descriptions. The reason is that I want the manager and the team members to "agree" that this document is the best way to achieve what the company is trying to accomplish.

I, again, like these to be one-page documents (2 at the absolute most) that clearly outline the tasks and duties of every position you have in your organizational structure. I have seen a 5-page long job description that management nor employee knew anything it said. We have free templates on our website for a tech-level, management-level, or C-level employee to get you started at www.chriscornelison.com. We also teach to write these and the main five documents in our two-day Super Culture™ classes.

More Templates Available

This isn't supposed to be complex. I rarely make any of these documents longer than one page. Keeping it simple helps ensure you and your team understand it enough to use it. Clear is kind.

For readers of this book, I have more templates to help you quickly complete these five documents. Visit www.chriscornelison.com or scan the QR code in the back of this book to download yours today.

More To Come...

We have covered **"Rule #1: It all starts with you"** in creating a Super Culture™, and now you have **"Rule #2: Write it down or it doesn't exist."** Now, we get to the really fun stuff! In the next chapter, I'll take you through Rule #3 and show you the surprising benefits of the power of praise.

Key Takeaways

✔ **If It's Not Written Down, It Doesn't Exist:** You can't just wing it. Writing things down gives your team clarity and direction. Without it, you'll be stuck in a culture driven by moods and inconsistency. Remember, "clear is kind."

✔ **Your Culture Document is the Foundation:** The culture document defines the environment of greatness you want to create. It's more than just core values—it sets the tone for how your team operates and gives leadership something to protect and enforce.

✔ **Five Key Documents Create a Super Culture™:** To build a Super Culture™, you need these five short documents: the culture document, company standards, vision document, organizational chart, and position agreements. Each one gives your team clear direction and purpose.

✔ Short and sweet. These 5 powerful documents should be as short as possible and almost always shorter than 1 page.

✔ **Leadership Styles Matter:** Knowing when to use the right leadership style is crucial. Coaching and visionary leadership will keep your team engaged, while command and control should only be used when absolutely necessary. Get the balance right, and your team will thrive.

✔ **It's a Living, Breathing Process:** These 5 documents aren't set in stone. They should grow and evolve as your company does. Don't be afraid to make changes, but make sure they're always written down so everyone stays on the same page. Keep them simple and keep them clear.

CHAPTER 5

Rule 3 – Praise What You Want Repeated™

"If you want to have a Super Culture you have to learn to Praise What You Want Repeated."

~Chris Cornelison

We have established Rule 1: It all starts with you and Rule 2: Write it down or it does not exist. Now, we are at Rule 3, which is my favorite one by far: If you want to have a Super Culture™, you must learn to Praise What You Want Repeated™.

A Leader's Most Powerful Tool

I believe that praise is the most powerful tool a leader has. It isn't reprimand, experience, rewards, yelling, or even bonuses; **IT IS PRAISE**. Praise is a superpower for leaders. Praise surprisingly brings a multitude of benefits when you utilize it correctly. It builds the confidence of your team and shows them you care.

PRAISE

- Improves culture
- Decreases workforce turnover
- Decreases reprimands
- Increases sales
- Increases implementation
- Promotes happiness
- Fosters employee pride
- Shows the team you care
- Increases employee confidence
- Makes people feel appreciated

Praise does two AMAZING THINGS!

First, it keeps people out of amygdala hijack (discussed in 3).

Second, it creates maximum focus.

People have an easy time understanding that there is a fight-or-flight side of the brain. Yet, they don't always understand that there is a praise side of the brain, too. This is a shame because the praise side of the brain is where the real Super Culture™ magic happens. The praise side enhances memory and learning and helps people become comfortable in their environment. I have a fun dog story that helps illustrate this concept. Then, we will explain the science of the praise side of the brain and emotional intelligence in a very simple way.

Kirby & My Hula Hoop

The best way I know to illustrate the power of praise is to introduce you to my Maltipoo Kirby and his hula hoop. When my family brought Kirby home, my wife and my daughter decided they wanted to teach Kirby how to jump through a hula hoop. I had no idea how to teach this dog to jump through a hoop, but I heard about people who trained dolphins and I had seen where the trainers would have the dolphins swim around the pool. As they went over the rope, the trainers gave them a fish. They repeated this until they jumped higher and higher.

So, I told my wife to hold the dog on one side of the hula hoop. I got some treats and I held a treat on the other side. Kirby has never seen a hoop before, so he isn't excited about it, but when he sees the treat, he starts scratching, clawing, yipping, and trying to get away and get that treat.

I held the hoop touching the ground and told my wife to let him go. He dashed through the hoop and grabbed the treat the very first time! Now, I know most of you reading this are thinking, "he didn't jump through the hoop because Chris had it touching the floor", and that would be correct.

But I remind you here we have to train our team before we expect them to leap to high heights.

After some more successes with the hoop on the ground, I raised the hoop and held the treat for Kirby to jump through the hoop and get the treat because **the goal was** to jump through the hoop. Kirby ran under the hoop, so I took the treat away. Just like in a Super Culture™, there is accountability. Kirby didn't jump the hoop so I didn't reward him with the treat.

We repeated this several more times, moving the hoop up and down so he would catch on, and you know what? On day one, after about 10-15 minutes of training, he jumped through that hoop.

At this point we had fed him too many treats, so we put the hoop away for day one. But I was super excited to try again when I got home the next day. I wanted to see how much Kirby remembered.

Day Two of Training Kirby

Kirby saw the hoop and immediately went crazy with excitement because he knew the hoop signified treats (This is similar to how a Super Culture™ document signifies a work environment of greatness). So, I held the hoop off the ground, my wife let him go, and Kirby went under the hoop; instead of jumping through it like I wanted.

Dang it! I wish I could say he jumped through it, but that wasn't what happened.

After a few failed attempts, I realized my dog was much like a corporate team, and he needed more coaching leadership because he wasn't trained up to the level I needed him to be yet. So, I moved the hoop back to the floor. I got him used to going through the hoop again, then slowly raised it up. And after about 5-10 minutes into day two, guess what? He started jumping through that hoop! He went through it multiple times, we all had a blast, and in two days, we trained Kirby to jump through the hoop.

Let's Do A Pretend Experiment With Kirby—BUT NO TREATS!

Let's say we go back to day one when Kirby had never seen this hula hoop before. He's not excited to see it when I get it out, and my wife doesn't have to hold him because he has no idea what this hoop is. I'll try to use command and control leadership to get him to jump through the hoop.

No treats. My wife doesn't hold him.

I simply raise the hoop off the ground and I scream, "JUMP THROUGH THE HOOP!" What do you think the chances are that this cute puppy jumps through the hoop now? Think back to Chapter 3, where we covered emotional intelligence and the amygdala hijack.

Let's take command and control leadership a step further here and add some adjectives. I try again, "Are you lazy? Are you a millennial? Are you a Gen Z? Have I not shown you how to do this over and over again? I SAID jump through the hoop, NOW!"

Let's be honest. The chances are much higher that this dog will poop on your floor than jump through the hoop if you yell at him like that.

My point here is definitely not to compare human beings to animals, but it is to grasp that our brains still function similarly when in amygdala hijack which is often caused inside a normal culture. In normal culture, leaders use the wrong style of leadership and get the wrong result from their efforts. They try to achieve something that wasn't written down, not trained for, and not praised at all, and they try to get results by using command and control leadership.

That One Time I Told This Story at the Coaching Clinic

I told this story during a keynote at the Mississippi Coaches Association on Leadership and The Power of Praise. Several very big football coaches were sitting in the front row and having a great time. They were really into the talk, but when I told Kirby's story, I noticed those previously engaged huge men were now sitting with their arms crossed.

I made eye contact with them and said, "I know what you are thinking. You are thinking, 'By gosh, I can make him go through that hoop!'" They nodded "yes," and we all had a laugh because that was *exactly* what they were thinking.

So I said "Okay, let's have it your way. Let's see what it looks like." I got into position, held the hoop, and said, "DANG IT I SAID JUMP THROUGH THE HOOP! And let's say the dog goes through the hoop. Let's say you're right. Sometimes, you could use command and control leadership at the wrong time and actually still get the results you want."

Then I say, "But let's put the hoop up on day one like I did before, and then let's get it back out on day two."

Now what do you think the dog will do? He's not excited to see the hoop. He's running the other way. You see, the hoop (which I'm referring to as your culture) now signifies nothing but yelling, torment, and lack of appreciation, which causes the people—both coaches and players, employees and management—to go into an amygdala hijack.

If this is the only way you train your team, players, employees, and customers, they will have their amygdala tripped just by simply walking in the front door of your locker room, your company, or your office. It could even happen when they hear your voice if all they associate your voice with is getting yelled at all the time. They will feel unappreciated, they will underperform, and they will leave when they get a chance.

A Third Scenario (No Treat and No Yelling)

Let's pretend we go back to day one, one last time, to train my Maltipoo, Kirby, and again, he has never seen the hoop. This last time, let's say there is no treat and no yelling at all. So I am not going to use any command and control leadership here.

It is day one, and he isn't excited because he has no idea what the hoop signifies. My wife doesn't have to hold him tight. I lift the hoop slightly off the ground, my wife lets him go, and we just sit and wait for him to jump the hoop. And we wait, and we wait, and we wait.

What do you think the chances of him just jumping through the hoop are? Really low, right? And what are the chances he loves it and does it over and over again? Just about zero, right? Readers, this is like expecting your team to leap to high heights of success and a great culture without ever writing anything down. Without anything written down, your team will just dangle in confusion, staying in constant chaos, and will produce underachieving results.

If you haven't taken anything from this book to this point, and you don't get anything else from this book, please get this:

"Animals starve for treats, people starve for praise."

"When praise goes up, the culture gets better."

You see, the dog went through the hoop over and over and over and loved it because animals starve for treats…..the people in your company are starving for praise. When I say starving, I mean STARVING! And I purposefully use that word because it has been proven that humans are addicted to praise.

I say this because electrodes have been hooked to human brains, and they show that the same areas that light up for caffeine, sugar, and cocaine are the same areas that light up for praise. That means every time you pat someone on the back, tell them, "Good job!", and you make them feel appreciated in any way,[5] their brain tells them this is good, they feel good, they repeat positive habits, and culture gets better.

In addition, when you Praise What You Want Repeated™ it makes it fun for you, too. Praise is the key to making everything fun for the leader and the team. Praise is the secret sauce to everything in a Super Culture™.

Praise Your Team Into Maximum Focus

The key to maximum focus is to get a chemical called acetylcholine to circulate in the brain. When acetylcholine is in the brain, learning is greatly enhanced, habits are created and habits will go into the memory much more quickly. When habits go into memory they are now a part of our "subconscious" that we discussed in Chapter 3 on emotional intelligence.

---

[5] "Scientific Explanation to Why People Perform Better after Receiving a Compliment." *ScienceDaily*, 2012, www.sciencedaily.com/releases/2012/11/121109111517.htm.

I hope you recall that the human subconscious is about 80 times faster than our conscious thinking. If we can create good habits in the subconscious, that is a very positive thing for the workforce and our Super Culture™! You have all seen a corporation that is just a well-oiled machine, and the people are great. I guarantee those companies will trace back to great leadership, written down documents, goals, and PRAISE.

But how do you get acetylcholine circulating in the brain?

First, learn how to manage and avoid amygdala hijack. When the amygdala fires, acetylcholine rushes out to the body to help contract muscles in case we have to fight or flight (from Chapter 3).

Second, you can increase acetylcholine circulating in the brain by learning to use three powerful leadership chemicals. You don't have to remember the names, but I'll walk you through a simple introduction to each one.

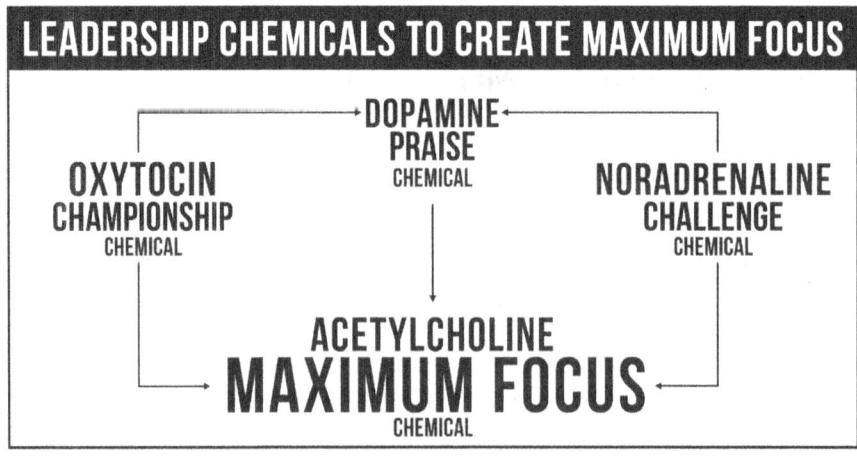

LEADERSHIP CHEMICALS TO CREATE MAXIMUM FOCUS

DOPAMINE
PRAISE
CHEMICAL

OXYTOCIN
CHAMPIONSHIP
CHEMICAL

NORADRENALINE
CHALLENGE
CHEMICAL

ACETYLCHOLINE
MAXIMUM FOCUS
CHEMICAL

Oxytocin: The Championship Chemical

Oxytocin is often called the love or touch chemical because it comes out through instances of touch, such as high fives and romantic touch, to name a few. Oxytocin comes really fast. It feels really good, but it goes away super fast. Now, I like to call oxytocin the championship chemical or the big-win chemical.

Stop here and close your eyes for about 30 seconds and think of a time when you won a championship. If you've never won a championship, think of something big—a birth, a wedding, graduation, something meaningful in your life where everything was great.

Now, picture all the vivid imagery you remember of that day. What were you wearing? What was the climate like? Who was there with you? What were the expressions on your face when that moment happened? How did you celebrate? Look at just how vividly you remember that day.

Now, think back to one year ago from the date you're reading this book. What do you remember about that day? Unless something very significant happened that day, you probably don't remember anything.

That is the power of oxytocin leading to acetylcholine and creating maximum focus.

The only problem is oxytocin doesn't usually lead straight to acetylcholine. Oxytocin goes away really fast and usually leads straight to dopamine.

Dopamine: The Praise Chemical

Most people call dopamine the happy chemical, which is why a lot of leadership experts say, "Give them a dopamine shot!"

The reason it's referred to as a shot is because it doesn't last very long either. Just a few seconds, but it does last a little bit longer than oxytocin. I like to call dopamine the praise chemical and the awesome thing about dopamine is it often relaxes our mood and almost always leads straight to acetylcholine in the brain!

You trigger dopamine anytime you praise somebody on your team. Anytime you give them a high five, you tell them thank you for showing up on time, you tell them "Way to go," you tell them that was a good pitch to the customer, or you make any positive comment! Anytime you praise your team, dopamine is released, and that leads to acetylcholine quickly after. This creates a calm, competent, and focused mindset where acetylcholine circulates in the brain, training is absorbed quickly, and good habits are formed really easily in those environments. MAXIMUM FOCUS!

Noradrenaline: The Challenge Chemical

I call noradrenaline the challenge chemical. Noradrenaline can be a precursor to adrenaline, which can trip your amygdala. I want to show you how this chemical can lead to maximum focus and how the chemical could trip the amygdala and shut your employee down.

Imagine that I'm walking to my house late at night. It's pitch black, and there's rustling in the bushes. Noradrenaline shoots into my brain, but it does not trip my amygdala right away. My eyes constrict and my heart rate goes up, and I am actually in maximum focus.

Then, a cat walks out. I'm happy to see a cat, so there's no adrenaline triggering my amygdala. I smile, dopamine is released, which leads straight to acetylcholine, and I walk into the house relaxed.

Now, let's picture a different scenario.

Let's say the bush rustles and a guy jumps out with a gun. My amygdala trips, and I'm either going to fight or flight. I am probably going to run. And that's when I would go into a hijack.

I call noradrenaline the challenge chemical because people who are adrenaline junkies and high achievers are usually extremely competitive. They absolutely have to have exciting goals and challenges to produce noradrenaline in their work environment. They need day-to-day challenges that cause noradrenaline to be released to get excited and to get fulfillment at work. So when they come in, you need good goals that are challenging, yet not so tough that they think they're going to fail each day. You want a challenging goal that makes them think, "I can do that. I see the path where my work is meaningful." "This is how we win the game!"

In these moments, noradrenaline leads straight to dopamine, then to acetylcholine, or it can lead straight to acetylcholine. Either way, it creates maximum focus!

You know what? I'm that super competitive, high-achiever type of guy. If the company I work for doesn't have challenging goals, they will eventually lose me. I have to go somewhere where I feel a sense of winning and purpose, somewhere I will feel appreciated and I can achieve greatness.

That's how the power of praise leads your team to get into maximum focus. I've taken you through the three chemicals and how they can trigger the flow of acetylcholine in the brain. You know what makes them work and how they work together. Praise is by far the easiest thing to generate dopamine, and dopamine is the easiest way to acetylcholine which leads to MAXIMUM FOCUS.

The chart below gives a day-to-day example.

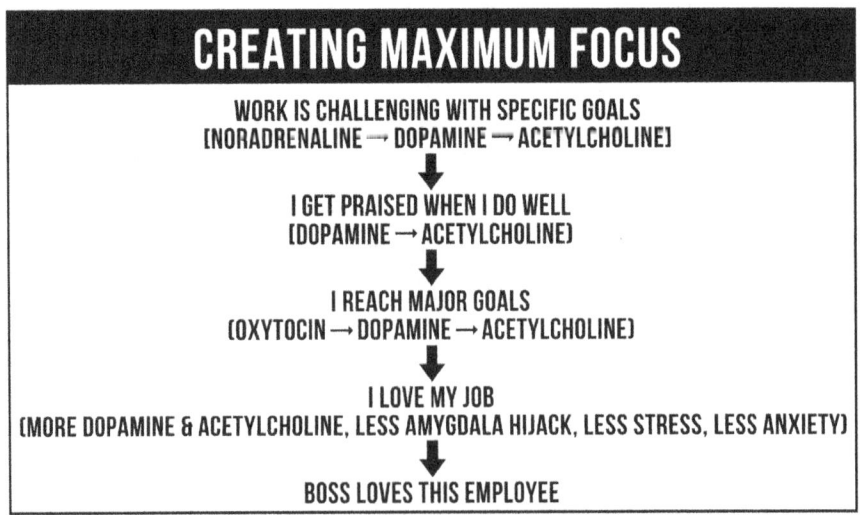

Examples of Maximum Focus In A Super Culture™ Environment

Example #1:

Employee walks in, and work is challenging with specific and visible quarterly goals. Noradrenaline is released into the brain. Noradrenaline usually leads to acetylcholine or dopamine, and dopamine leads to acetylcholine then to maximum focus.

Example #2:

An employee is praised for doing well. Dopamine is immediately released into the brain, which leads to the release of acetylcholine and then leads to maximum focus.

Example #3:

Employee or team reaches a major or quarterly goal. Oxytocin leads to dopamine or acetylcholine, which leads to maximum focus.

Example #4:

Employee loves their job as soon as they walk in the front door, someone smiles and says, "Good morning," and dopamine is released first thing in the morning. Acetylcholine is released immediately because they're not stressed out in their environment, and they prepare for an awesome day of work inside their Super Culture™.

Praise Equity

There is one more Major benefit to praise. I call it **Praise Equity**. As praise goes up it causes the amygdala to be fired less. The amygdala has been proven to shrink a little over time and become less sensitive the less it is fired, which leads to less stress and anxiety on a day-to-day basis. This builds up equity with your employees like equity in a bank. When we talk about accountability later, having praised enough creates Praise Equity so your employees don't "shut down" so easily when you have to coach and hold accountability. Praise equity lets people know the leader cares. If they hear 10 praises before they hear criticism, they are much less likely to take it personally and shut down into an amygdala hijack.

Praise plays a crucial part in elevating your environment out of normal culture. Praise What You Want Repeated™ on your path toward creating a Super Culture™. Don't overthink it. When in doubt, praise it out.

A Testimonial For The Power of Praise

Hi Chris,

Thank you again for coming and speaking to us. I have gotten some really good feedback from the staff on how much they learned and enjoyed your training.

Participating in Super Culture™ training was a turning point for me as an HR manager, teaching me that the journey to a positive workplace culture starts with my own actions and leadership. The training highlighted the importance of active listening and the power of employee praise, empowering me to lead by example and embody our organization's core values every day. Since implementing these strategies, I've witnessed a significant uplift in team engagement and morale. This experience has not only improved my effectiveness in my role but also underscored the impact of personal leadership in fostering a supportive and dynamic work environment.

Thank you again.

Morgan Robinson
HR Manager & Trainer
Telco Community Credit Union

Specific Praise Is The Key To Everything

All praise counts, but the **more specific** it is, the more powerful it becomes because it also creates a positive habit. If you want your culture to improve, praise things that improve your culture, like being on time, following processes correctly, executing strategy toward goals, and smiling first thing in the morning, and you'll improve your culture. If you want workplace turnover to decrease, praise more, and turnover will decrease. Praise is the key to reducing reprimands and the key to increasing sales. It is the key to hitting the quarterly goals. You praise the things you want repeated.

Want to bring those five documents to life? Hold everyone accountable to them and praise them when they get it right! Specific praise is the best way to use Coaching Style Leadership because you are giving them the "whys" as you praise.

PRAISE COINS

I believe in the power of praise so deeply that a couple of decades ago I created a training tool I call a Praise Coin to train managers and leaders on my team. The coin has my mantra printed on it, "Praise What You Want Repeated™", and in the middle says "Praise 10X a day." This is significant because I want my managers to praise 10 times a day minimum. I even put it on the tasks and duties section of their position agreement to praise their team 10 times or more daily.

The way it works is you simply put the coin in your pocket as a daily reminder to "praise what you want repeated." These are all the little things your team does to achieve the quarterly goals, fulfill the vision, go the extra mile, execute their position well, and for sure create the Super Culture™. Anytime a leader puts this coin in their pocket and their praise goes up, Super Culture™ accelerates!

Making praise part of your company policy does two things:

1. Praise is the key to making people feel appreciated and decreasing workforce turnover.
2. Holding managers accountable to praising also holds the managers accountable themselves to coach toward the goals of the company (we'll look at this more in Chapter 6).

Often, managers ask what to praise. I say "ANYTHING you want repeated. Preferably things that strengthen our culture, fulfill our goals, and make people know you appreciate what they do for our team and company."

The minute you take a management position at my company, the number one thing on your tasks and duties in your position agreement becomes to protect our culture. The number two thing on your task and duties list is praise ten times a day.

Ten times is significant to me. The number one reason for this is that you should praise 10 times a day to build that Praise Equity before you have to hold somebody accountable for something.

When you praise people, you build Praise Equity in the sound of your voice and on walking through the front door. You don't want your office to trip the amygdala. When they're used to hearing good things, you empower them to learn and improve in a safe environment.

Now, when you need to hold a team member accountable and say, "Hey, Chris, you didn't get that exactly right, we need you to do it this way because it's faster," it is much less likely to trip their amygdala. The acetylcholine stays floating in their brain, and they quickly put the knowledge you've given them into forming a new better habit.

When you trade 10 praises for every reprimand, Praise Equity works to help build the Super Culture™ you want. I hold my managers accountable to praising ten times a day minimum. I really want 50 times a day, better yet, a hundred times a day, to put that Praise Equity in the bank with all of their direct reports.

When team members know that you appreciate them and that you notice those little things they do every day for the good of the company, they will start to get the little things exactly right. For example, they show up on time every day, are well-dressed, and do all the things that make your company successful. They support your core values, which support your culture.

The 10X also has another significant meaning I train managers with. You want to praise 10 times for every reprimand you have to give. So it is PRAISE, PRAISE, PRAISE, PRAISE, PRAISE, PRAISE, PRAISE, PRAISE, PRAISE, PRAISE,.... REPRIMAND.

A Testimonial For The Praise Coins

I did use the praise coin to help Jill (Pharmacy Manager) understand how she needs to give more praise rather than just criticism. The coin helped her understand the idea pretty well.

1. It definitely forced me to give more positive feedback, which became more natural and genuine. Before, it was not normal, so most of my feedback felt fake.

2. Something to track objectively. Praise coins help me track my positive feedback vs. negative feedback.

3. I have definitely changed my behavior to give more positive feedback. In fact, I feel as if I am giving more praise than criticizing, which makes me feel more comfortable.

Dipak Patel CEO
The Medicine Shop
Reading, Pennsylvania

Throughout my career, managers have come to me and said, "Chris, I'm not sure I want to praise 10 times a day. I'm not sure I want to give those small praises." It's not because they don't want to let their people know they're appreciated. It is because they are afraid their praise will seem insincere and not genuine. Also, praise is uncomfortable for some leaders in the beginning because this concept is rarely taught and it will be a new habit for a lot of leaders.

So, how do I answer them? Let me share a story I share with them that will help you understand how praising more often is such a huge benefit to your culture.

Let's say our company has a sales initiative to increase XYZ widget sales by 150 over the next quarter. That means the employee will have to make roughly 50 sales a month or two sales a day.

We have projected that we will be told no by the customer nine out of ten times in the beginning and when we get good it will be six out of ten times. So, our team must train, role-play, get the right things in place to execute the sale, and then actually educate a customer, which is going to be really awkward at first. Don't forget, they will get turned down a lot in the beginning before we start to make the sales.

They're going to get told no nine out of ten times, but we expect them to continue to execute the process every time so we can meet our sales goals. When they get told no, you want them to do it again. Over and over and over, every day for 90 days with no acknowledgment, no support, no praise.

There's no "Way to go!" but you expect them to keep doing this and keep hearing those "no's" with no praise at the end. Then you are going to catch the 150th sale in real-time, and confetti's going to shoot out. And you are going to run down to them and give them the "BIG THANK YOU!"

That doesn't make much sense, does it?

The Big Thank You is Nothing but a Big Myth!

The main problem with the Big Thank You is that it actually rarely comes. If leaders and managers avoid praise because they are not used to it, this leaves employees feeling underappreciated, and not motivated, and they begin to fail really quickly with no coaching support.

You have to praise them when they do the training, praise them when they role-play, praise them when they make that first awkward pitch to a client and get told "no." You praise them when they get told no because you want them to repeat it again.

You want them to get better at it. You praise the first sale too. You praise the second sale. It takes 90 days to create a habit, so any good manager has to focus on any new project every day for at least 90 days to properly train the team and get them to create new habits. Whether it's for the Super Culture™ or, as in this case, a sales goal for 90-day periods.

This Builds Praise Equity!

In the next chapter, we'll discuss when you have to hold them accountable. You'll see how this buildup of Praise Equity doesn't allow their amygdala to fire as easily, and they stay in maximum focus accomplishing exactly what you want them to do.

If you would like to order praise coins for your team, visit www.chriscornelison.com or scan the QR code in the back of the book.

Key Takeaways

✔ **Praise is the Most Powerful Tool a Leader Has:** It's not reprimands, rewards, or bonuses that make the biggest difference—it's praise. When used correctly, praise can completely transform a culture by making your team feel appreciated, boosting their confidence, and showing them you care. Praise what you want repeated!

✔ **Praise Builds Positive Habits:** Just like how I taught my dog Kirby to jump through a hula hoop with treats and encouragement, people respond to praise. When you reinforce the behaviors you want to see repeated, your team will keep delivering them. It's all about positive reinforcement—making the right actions a habit.

✔ **Praise Fuels Emotional Intelligence and Maximum Focus:** Praise triggers chemicals in the brain like dopamine and acetylcholine, which help your team feel confident and focused. A praised team is a productive team, ready to hit their goals with energy and enthusiasm.

✔ **Build Praise Equity:** Consistent praise builds up "Praise Equity," meaning when it comes time to offer constructive feedback, your team is much less likely to shut down or feel attacked. You've already established trust and appreciation, so they're more open to hearing how they can improve.

✔ **Skip the Myth of the Big Thank You:** Don't wait for a grand moment to show appreciation. Celebrate the small wins every day. From the first awkward pitch to nailing a big sale, praise along the journey keeps people motivated and ensures success.

CHAPTER 6

Rule 4 – Hold It Accountable

"The biggest misconception of culture is the it's all 'Rah, Rah!'".
Culture is not all 'Rah, Rah!'"

~Chris Cornelison

Our Culture Is Great, But The Team Is Not Hitting Any Goals

I have lost count of the number of people who have walked up to me over the years saying, "Hey, Chris. You know my company's doing great with our culture but we're just not hitting any of our goals."

That's an oxymoron to me. That is not Super Culture™. There is accountability to a Super Culture™. It's not just "I enjoy what I'm doing." That goes back to Chapter 4, where we talked about how you can have fun and be happy at work on social media or making paper airplanes, but that isn't what a Super Culture™ is all about. You can have fun on Facebook, Instagram, or any social media, but a Super Culture™ has fun while executing the duties, tasks, and responsibilities it takes to hit our goals and drive the company forward.

Honestly, what I think when I hear people say this is they are avoiding daily accountability on the management level of the organizational chart.

Avoiding daily accountability is one of the biggest mistakes you can make as a leader of your company or team.

Everything Rises And Falls On Leadership, Praise, And Accountability

It starts with you being aware that there is a problem. You lead a person to improve by NOT shutting them down while still holding them accountable, AND you give them the "why" you want them to do something a different way.

This creates clarity, makes things go better, and does not shut their amygdala down because of the praise equity you've built up (refer back to Chapter 5 - Rule 3: Praise What You Want Repeated™).

Daily accountability cannot be pushed under the rug. Leaders cannot let accountability go when employees are clearly not following the culture and clearly not executing the daily steps it takes to fulfill the vision and hit the goals of the company. When you, as the manager or leader, allow behavior that goes against your culture to continue, it keeps happening until you explode into your own amygdala hijack, and fall into using command and control leadership at the wrong times. This drags your team culture down quickly.

Emotional intelligence allows you to become aware, change reactions, and get a different outcome. It will enable you to pause and consider taking a new direction with your reactions. The only way to change outcomes is to react differently.

The hardest part about accountability is accepting that it starts with you. When you write down a culture document, everyone expects the leader to get it right ten times in a row before they buy into it. Then leadership has to protect the Super Culture™ by holding everyone else accountable to it also.

Super Culture™ Praises While Maintaining Accountability

Super Culture™ praises ten times a day AND also encompasses accountability to all the written documents and the environment. The team has to choose their attitude, so they're accountable for the attitude they bring each day. Management must protect the culture with accountability and the proper vocabulary. This means you praise and reprimand with those very powerful 3-4 lines on your Super Culture™ document. You must reprimand and hold accountability within your position agreements and all the documents you have written down to create your Super Culture™. Let's look at a couple of examples.

Example #1:

Let's say I see an employee dealing with a really rude customer. The employee keeps their cool, doesn't get mad, and solves the customer's problem without making things worse.

I praise that employee for four things:

1. For choosing to stay calm, even when the customer was not.
2. For following the processes we laid out.
3. For solving the problem.
4. For moving on with the rest of the day with a positive attitude.

I just praised that employee four times for things directly from our culture document: choosing a great attitude, staying with their position agreement, staying happy, and being accountable to our goals.

It only took 15 seconds, and it wasn't generic praise because it came right from the culture document. This process gave the employee the "whys." I praised what I wanted to be repeated.

Now, let's take it further and say the patient was angry because we didn't do what we said we would. I also have to remind this same employee that we didn't perform our task the way our position agreement in the policy and procedure manual said, and we need attention so that it doesn't keep happening, and customers are not mad.

This is how there could be four to five praises and one constructive criticism in one very quick interaction, all of which can be found inside the Super Culture™ documents. The culture gets stronger! The employee is appreciated.

Example #2:

Let's say we set a goal to capture 100 sales of a widget.

- Our team trains and roleplays to improve the process. Management praises this effort.

- Then, someone on the team finds the right opportunity, offers the widget, and gets turned down. Management praises that team member for offering the widget because we want them to try again and we are praising what we want repeated.

- Then, someone makes the first sale of the widget. Management definitely praises this accomplishment with enthusiasm.

We keep praising what we want to be repeated, and this process repeats with different team members. We all get better and faster until we hit the goal of capturing 100 sales of that widget.

How different would it have been if we never praised the training, the roleplay, the preparation, the attempts when we fail, the early successes, the consistency of daily focus, and every step of the process? We would likely fail to hit our sales goal. There is accountability "to praise" in a Super Culture™.

You Cannot Skip Accountability

The big thing most cultures lack is accountability. Accountability has to become who you and your managers are every day. Just like praise!

Rule 1: It all starts with you.

Even accountability starts with you. I refer to what I call The Cornelison Rules of 10™:

- 10 praises for every constructive criticism
- 10 praises per day (minimum)
- 10 times the leader has to show they can improve before they can challenge the team to improve

It All Started With Me

Let's go back to my story in the beginning. When I was yelling and kicking garbage cans, my team didn't make a one-day turnaround because I wrote a culture document. They waited to see if "I" was going to change. Leaders serve others by going first—it all starts with you. So I had to "choose to be happy" 10 times in a row when each employee saw me in a situation where I used to throw a fit. That is what it takes to get team buy-in.

My team needed to see me NOT get irate ten times. Early on in my career, when we got busy and backed up, I would get mad and kick the garbage can in. I shut my team down. They needed to see a customer get rude with me; they needed to see us get backed up; they needed to see challenging situations that used to make me shut down and kick the garbage can, AND see me react differently inside our new Super Culture™ to believe that I changed and that I would no longer shut down and yell and fuss and cuss all day.

It all starts with you, just like it all started with me. I had to be accountable before I expected them to be accountable. That's why I truly believe there is no Kool-Aid.

There Is No Kool-Aid

Posters and quotes are awesome in the beginning, but leadership and accountability are what make a culture stand the test of time. I love to see a Super Culture™ poster up in a business that has been through my training or heard my keynote. But, I hate the concept of "drink the Kool-Aid." They say that you have to get everybody to drink the Kool-Aid. I agree that you do need buy-in at the beginning, but when the Kool-Aid is gone, we want to have created a new environment.

Normal cultures get pumped up for a couple days but lose accountability and consistency and that is why they fail. The key to Super Culture™ is consistency. Consistent praise, consistent accountability, consistent improvement, and consistency toward goals are how we make our Super Culture™ last forever (more coming on this in the next chapter).

The Cornelison Rules of 10™ state that the leader has to show they can improve 10 times before they can challenge the team to improve. They are waiting to see you respond differently in the heat of fire. Just like my team did with me, they need to actually see you improve 10 times. It may take you 20 times to get it right for each team member to actually see those 10 times and believe you have truly changed, but when they see it and believe it, then they will have long-term buy-in and actually participate in helping protect it, too.

The Daily Huddle

A useful tool for supporting the praise and accountability of a Super Culture™ is the Daily Huddle. The daily huddle, or morning huddle, since it happens first thing in the day, should be one to two minutes long. Rarely should it be over two minutes, and never, ever over five minutes. It's not a team meeting, it is a team huddle.

Someone should take notes in the huddle for your other shifts; AI apps will do this for you. The highest-ranking person on the team always leads it, and it happens every day unless there's an actual team meeting that day.

The Daily Huddle focuses on four goals:

1. Providing a positive start to the day.
2. Bringing awareness to anything that needs addressing from the day before (hopefully not often)
3. Praise the previous day's accomplishments toward quarterly goals.
4. Provide motivation and focus toward the quarterly goals that day, and always end on a positive note.

The Daily Huddle actually holds management accountable for coaching the team first thing every morning. It also holds management accountable for praise, accountability, and daily focus. This short 2 minutes a day creates amazing consistency in your team….and yes, you have 1-2 minutes a day to set your team up for success no matter how busy your company is.

For a step-by-step process of running successful Daily Huddles, visit www.chriscornelison.com or scan the QR code at the back of this book.

There are three main reasons Managers and Leaders fail to Hold it Accountable:

1. Lack of Trust
2. Fear of Conflict
3. Lack of Clarity.

First, let's look at **"lack of trust and fear of conflict."** I don't think this could be said any better than the great author Patrick Lencioni said it in the book *The Five Dysfunctions of a Team*. I am going to give a very short few lines of overview of a great book.

The foundation of a team in the book is trust. Therefore, the biggest problem laid out in the book is a "lack of trust" that *leads* to a "fear of conflict." Where I think a lot of people miss the point is that this trust isn't that I think you are a bad person or may steal from me. This trust is on a basic level that most companies (operating in Normal Culture) don't trust that they can make a suggestion, ask for clarity, or ask to do things differently, without management attacking them and their personal character.

There is also a fear from the management level that they can't hold accountability because they don't "trust" the employees or team members will not attack the manager and their personal character. So, problems go on and on every day, and the team never addresses anything, never hits goals, and never has the critical conversations it takes to pull out the greatness of their team and company.[6]

Now, let's look at **"lack of clarity."** The other reason managers don't hold accountability is a lack of clarity! "They don't have anything written down" therefore no real clarity exists. There is no position agreement or job description to let employees know what a good job looks like. There are no goals clearly posted for the team to work toward, and there is no Super Culture™ document to define the environment of greatness we want to work inside. Without these documents there is no common verbiage for the team and management, and therefore no consistency.

Without trust and clarity through the 5 Simple Rules of Super Culture™, these very important conversations to keep the team on track are usually avoided and below-par standards are accepted. No praise goes out, and the culture reverts back to a Normal Culture where no one has pride, no one is appreciated, and the company starts to fail.

---

[6] *Five Dysfunctions Products | the Table Group*. www.tablegroup.com/product/dysfunctions/.

Let's See What This Could Look Like:

A company with a Normal Culture tells its team they have a great new product and wants them to sell 150 of this new product in the next 90 days. The product will generate $25 per sale. It is a great product and there is training. But this company has no vision document, no job descriptions, and no culture document written down. They also fail to write the goal of 150 down (because the boss has already told them once). There is no plan to praise the progress and usually the goal is not talked about again. The boss never serves the team anymore, no one is in charge, no one steps up, and at the end of 90 days, the goal is not even close to being achieved. Often no one even acknowledges that the goal was missed! The company with a Normal Culture makes 10 total sales toward the goal and generates $250 of new revenue. They don't even know why they failed and they lower the goal to 20 the next quarter and probably won't even hit that. They are not happy, they feel unappreciated, and they are failing.

* * *

A company with a Super Culture™ has a vision document that says they are going to increase sales in new areas this year and this new product fits the vision. They train the team and then take the steps to prepare for the quarter. They post a goal poster in the back of the company for 150 sales this quarter for the whole team to see. They update the goal sheet every day and tell the team the progress toward the goal every morning in the Daily Huddle. They praise every step of the success and journey all 90 days. The company with a Super Culture hits the goal of 150 sales in 45 days, does over 215 sales for the quarter, and generates $5,375. They are preparing to raise the goal for the next quarter to

250 sales because they know they can do it! This company is happy, profitable, and in the top 10% of their industry.

Two Accountability Conversations

Coaching Conversation Versus Critical Conversation

A coaching conversation happens in the flow of the workday. A coaching conversation is short, quick, and to the point, whether it is praising or holding accountability. It is positive and it is to praise the action the manager wants repeated or to improve an action to better serve the team. It always gives the "why," whether it is praise or constructive criticism. It should use the verbiage of one of the five documents discussed earlier in Chapter 4 as often as possible. It should be a motivating conversation, both when praising and when holding accountability.

A critical conversation occurs when an employee is making the same mistakes over and over again, or violating Company Standards. It should be in a private area like an office. It may have or need some documentation to read and agree on, and it probably needs some documentation for improvement.

Both of these conversations are accountability conversations. Coaching conversations should happen all day, every day. Critical conversations are only as needed.

Coaching Conversation Example:

If you work at Chick-fil-A, the process is for their team to respond to everybody with, "My pleasure." If you're the manager and you see a server miss this, you need to have that coaching conversation with them.

You: "Hey, Rob, you did great. You followed our process to a T, and they left with a great smile, except you forgot to say our slogan of 'My pleasure.'"

Rob responds with: "Yeah, I forgot..."

You encourage him: "No worries. Next customer!"

As the manager, you watch Rob's next conversations to see if he gets it right. You're not watching him to see if he gets it wrong. Great coaches watch to see them getting it right so they can praise it. The biggest mistake people make with coaching conversations is when the person gets it right, the manager neglects to praise them.

When Is A Conversation Critical?

Maybe an employee is coming in late every day, and you've already discussed it twice. Maybe you've already followed your company's process for writing them up. This conversation requires more firmness, troubleshooting, and patience on the manager's part.

With my employees, this conversation happens in the office, where we can be alone and quiet. I will walk them through exactly where it is written down and what they are violating. I will also tell them exactly what we need them to do to improve and be a part of our team. This conversation cannot be a personal attack, and even critical conversations should be executed with the same integrity your Super Culture™ document states, even when it gets to the point of firing the employee.

You truly want to make an effort to help them be a productive part of the team. So, during these critical conversations, I often ask, "How can I help you be happy at work?" Many times, an employee will opt out of it with, "No, no, I'm happy." That's when I remind them that culture goes both ways, and I must "Be Happy" too. Their performance is not making me happy.

Obviously, you have to get the verbiage right for the current situation, but it looks something like this: "I have to be happy, too. And, as your manager, when you yell and slam things and the customer can see it, cuss out loud on the way out, and slam the door behind you, that makes me unhappy."

Sometimes you need to coach people up inside of a Super Culture™, and sometimes you need to coach them out of your Super Culture™ so you do not run off your great employees, which I refer to as Eagles in the next chapter. You also have to protect the culture at all times, which we get into in the next chapter.

Do's And Don'ts For A Super Culture™

Things to Nurture In A Super Culture™: Do's

- ✓ Praise loud. Reprimand quietly.
- ✓ Praise 10 times a day.

- ✓ Praise what you want repeated. Culture, wins, goals, etc.
- ✓ As the leader, pat yourself on the back for praising.
- ✓ As a leader, pat yourself on the back for holding accountability (that is still serving the team's culture).
- ✓ Do have a Daily Huddle.
- ✓ Do have Coaching and Critical Conversations.

Things To Avoid In A Super Culture™: DON'Ts

- ✗ Don't let leaders avoid accountability. If the leader avoids accountability over and over, it eventually explodes and destroys the culture.
- ✗ Don't let things become personal and attacking. When the leader lets this enter the culture, trust is violated, and the employee goes into an amygdala hijack and shuts down (I teach more about how to avoid this in my classes).

It starts with you honoring what you wrote down. For me, it starts with always being happy and having fun at work. Once you have that, you're ready to move into protecting and thriving in your culture, which I will take you through in the next chapter.

My classes help your company leaders understand accountability and how to have those conversations more effectively. If you would like to check them out, go to www.chriscornelison.com or scan the QR code at the back of this book.

Key Takeaways

✓ **Accountability Strengthens the Culture:** It's not all about "rah-rah" fun. If you're not hitting goals, that's not a Super Culture™. Accountability means holding everyone to what's been written down—no avoiding it. You can't just have a happy workplace without making sure people are getting their work done, too.

✓ **Praise and Accountability Go Hand in Hand:** You've got to praise people to build them up, but you also need to hold them accountable to keep them on track. Leaders have to balance the two—Praise What You Want Repeated™ and address what needs fixing. It's not about being harsh; it's about making sure everyone's moving toward the same goal.

✓ **It Starts with You:** Your team isn't going to buy into the culture if they don't see you living it every day. They're waiting to see if you've really changed, just like my team waited on me. You have to show up differently ten times in a row before they'll believe the change is real.

✓ **The Daily Huddle is a Simple Tool with a Big Impact:** Two minutes every morning to praise yesterday's wins, address any issues, and set the focus for the day. It's simple, quick, and powerful for keeping your team on the right path.

✓ **Handle Critical Conversations Right:** When someone's off track, you have to address it, but do it the right way. Don't make it personal or attack their character—stick to the facts, give them the "whys," and show them you're invested in helping them improve.

This is how you build a Super Culture™ that lasts!

CHAPTER 7

Rule 5 – Protect & Thrive

"We must protect this house!"

~Under Armour

Once you create a Super Culture™, you protect it by hiring, training, and firing, and you thrive in it by hitting goals and rewarding inside it.

Hiring

Hiring is never a perfect science, but when you have a process and written documents to use, it gets easier and much more consistent. It's just another benefit of having a Super Culture™.

Let me share our process. It starts by giving the candidate two very important pieces of paper: a one-page position agreement to tell them exactly what the duties, tasks, and responsibilities of the position they are applying for require, and our Super Culture™ document that tells them the exact environment of greatness we want our company to thrive in.

Then, we have two interviewers ask specific questions based on those two documents. We ask open-ended questions about a scenario that fits the position. We give them a problem and ask how they would handle it. We let the candidate answer the question. Then, after they answer it we take away the answer they gave. For example, if they answer "I would get my manager," then we say, "What if your manager wasn't in the office? What would you do then?" We want to make them think and get them talking so we can figure out if their answers make them a fit for our Super Culture™ and if they can meet the tasks and responsibilities of the position. When we finish with the interview, we thank them for coming and tell them we will follow up in 7-10 days. We spend about 5-10 minutes discussing the candidate immediately after the interview.

We bring the candidates back that we want to hire for a second interview. We do follow up with an email to other candidates respectfully telling them we have hired another candidate and thanking them for their interest.

We rarely hire any position without interviewing at least three candidates, and we always bring a candidate back for a second interview before we hire.

The written documentation of a one-page position agreement and a Super Culture™ document GREATLY improves the level of candidates you hire and greatly increases the chance of hiring proper fits into your company Super Culture™.

In a Super Culture™ interview, you are looking for the skills required for the position and the attitude that will fit into your culture and make it grow.

Training

I am often amazed at the lack of training programs in all companies (even my own when I was kicking that can, LOL), especially in businesses with less than 100 employees. This lack of training is probably because of a lack of written documents, most likely position agreements or job descriptions. This lack of training leads to what I call the Honeymoon Phase.

Honeymoon Phase

THE HONEYMOON PHASE

- ALMOST EVERY EMPLOYEE IS GREAT FOR THE FIRST FEW WEEKS.
- THIS IS THE TIME TO GET 10 PRAISES A DAY IN, AND GIVE THEM THE "WHYS" ON WHAT THEY DON'T KNOW YET.
- IF THE MANAGER DOESN'T TRAIN DURING THE HONEYMOON PHASE, THE EMPLOYEE WILL FADE AFTER 30 DAYS AND BE STUCK!

Almost every employee is great the first few weeks of a new job they take on. I believe they come in and genuinely want to do a good job. Early in my career, I had countless times that employees would hire into our company and everyone on the team would tell me how good of an employee they were going to be, sometimes even saying they were the best we ever hired—only to come in within two to four weeks and complain that the same employee isn't cutting it.

The Honeymoon Phase is that initial two to six-week period where a new employee is like a sponge and has a great work ethic. They do everything you ask, exactly like you ask. There is no way for them to learn everything they need to know in this short period of time.

This is the time to get 10-50 praises in and be aware that you are building Praise Equity every day. It is also the time to become aware of the things they do not know how to do yet—for example, priority of what to do next, how to do things faster, safer, or better.

This is the time for training. If you are not aware of this, every employee will start to fade around the 30-day mark, the Honeymoon Phase will be over, and you will be stuck in a normal culture forever.

The main reason most companies do not train is that they have a lack of written down documents, processes, and goals. You, as the reader of this book, know better and have 5 one-page documents that can change all of that! We have talked about the documents it takes, how to praise, and how to hold them accountable. Now, I am going to give you a super simple training process.

This is my training process. You can copy it or feel free to change it to fit into your company.

TRAINING YOUR TEAM

DAY 1

1. READ YOUR POSITION AGREEMENT, CULTURE DOCUMENT, AND RELATIVE PARTS OF THE POLICY & PROCEDURE MANUAL
2. LEARN COMPUTER SOFTWARE, TRAINING CLASSES, AND VIDEOS
3. PAIR WITH PROPER RANKING PERSON IN THEIR DEPARTMENT

DAY 8, 15, 30

- READ POSITION AGREEMENT WITH MANAGER AGAIN
- MANAGER COACHES THE POSITION AGREEMENT, GOALS, AND ANY PROCESSES THAT NEED ATTENTION
- A GOOD MANAGER WILL GIVE "WHYS"
- BI-ANNUAL REVIEWS EVERY 6 MONTHS AFTER FIRST 30 DAYS

On Day 1

On day one, the new employee reads their position agreement and the culture document. These are both one-page documents. That person will also be required to read the relevant parts of the policy and procedures manual with their direct report, a manager, or at least with correspondence from a manager. I expect the manager to show every new employee what parts of the policy and procedures manual correspond to their position.

The new employee will receive any computer classes, manuals, and other digital, verbal, or written materials that they need to fulfill the duties and responsibilities of the position they take.

Putting Them in the Pocket of Another Employee

Lastly, on day one, we will pair the new employee with a proper ranking person in their department. This is a person we consider an eagle because they are great at their job, and we'll put that new employee "in their pocket." The new hire will shadow this current great employee, and I challenge this person to give the new employee the "whys" for everything, especially our culture. We don't assume they know anything. They likely come from a Normal Culture and we do not want *any* of that to bleed over into our Super Culture™.

This shadowing does something special to the Eagle or upper-level current employee. It holds the upper-level employee accountable to the growth and protection of our culture. It praises the existing employee for being the standard that we want. For the new employee, it allows them to have a specific contact person other than their manager who has a high standard that we would like them to strive for.

Days 8, 15, and 30

This training continues on days 8, 15, and 30. This is the real sweet sauce of our training process. Most companies, if they even train on day 1, *never train any further*. We let every new employee know that on days 8, 15, and 30, they will go over their position agreement again with the manager, and they will have the opportunity to ask any questions about things they don't understand. We hold the managers accountable to meeting on days 8, 15, and 30 to set up team members for success and not be stuck in the Honeymoon Phase.

This process holds our managers accountable to spend more time training our new team members on things they might have missed, not understood, been doing unsafely, not up to production speed, etc. It also allows new employees to ask questions in a scheduled sit-down meeting with their direct report. It holds both the manager and the new employee accountable for the process to protect our culture. This part of the process eliminates the Honeymoon Phase.

On those days, the manager mainly coaches the position agreement, goals, and any processes that need attention. Nobody gets it all right at the beginning. Most companies fail to tell the employee clearly what they want them to do (see Chapter 4, Write it down), therefore the employee fades into mediocrity and Normal Culture because managers in Normal Cultures fail to coach after day 1.

After day 30, you can roll into your company's ordinary bi-annual review process. But now you have a very well-trained employee who is still moving forward and therefore strengthening your Super Culture™.

This process also eliminates the Honeymoon Phase and sets the whole team up to protect the Super Culture™ of greatness we all want. New employees will actually have a huge advantage over older employees because the training and documents get better and better as the company grows.

Super Culture™ is always growing, nurturing, training, and getting better. That's why longevity with the company is never a big factor in the quality of an employee and why a good employee is always looked at from an asset point of view. What is important to the organization is how well a team member can do their job and how well they can help others do their job.

> Everyone inside a company is either an asset or a liability to the company. You are an asset if you bring in more resources to the company than you cost the company. If you cost the company more resources than you bring in, then you're a liability.

That may sound harsh, but everybody inside a company, including me, is an asset or a liability to the company. Experience and longevity are not the same thing. Experience is valuable and meaningful because of things an employee has learned and helped create; therefore, they are more experienced and can do things better and faster than a new employee, which makes them a great asset. Longevity just means the employee was there for a period of time, not necessarily that they got better over time.

Firing

I hate to fire people, and every firing feels like, and is, a personal failure on some level. However, I've done it several times and will do it again to protect our culture. I wish I could tell you that you won't have to fire anybody on your existing team, but that is rarely the case. Once a Super Culture™ is established, firing goes down because hiring and training are much better.

But the truth is that during the transition from a Normal Culture to a Super Culture™, some people will just not accept the new way of thinking. At this point, you're faced with only two decisions: either fire your turkeys or be prepared to lose your

Eagles. Turkeys are the employees that are subpar to what your company requires to get the job done. Eagles are the ones soaring high and getting things done to hit the goals.

Eagles don't like working with turkeys inside of Super Culture™. You give a turkey as many chances as possible to be coached inside this new environment and acknowledge that the old environment was not their fault. I had to fire people when I changed the culture of my company and I actually apologized to a couple of people.

I said, "I know the reason you can't get on board is my failed leadership earlier in my career. I know why you don't believe in the new direction we are headed and why you can't buy in. I know you're going to be great somewhere else."

So, you still fire within your Super Culture™ because Eagles don't like to work with turkeys. Protecting the culture is not about the turkeys. You cannot let the behavior of one individual violate the culture. Everyone sees it, and it will destroy your culture (see Chapter 6: Rule 4 - Hold It Accountable).

If you let a turkey stick around too long, it doesn't just affect that person and you—it affects every employee on your team and every family member of your team. When you decide not to hold accountability for one employee, you literally choose to hurt hundreds more.

When I have to fire people, I have a set process I follow that I'll share with you now. I tell them exactly why they're being let go, give them a severance, and I am done with the conversation in less than five minutes. Anything over five minutes means you personally feel bad about something and it is of no benefit to the employee being fired—don't go over five minutes.

If they want to talk afterward, I'll listen to them. However, while I listen, I mentally picture every member of my team and every member of their families popping up around them. I know I made a decision within our culture to protect the good of the whole team, and we move forward.

When I started this book, I told you a story of how I made my employees miserable, and I am not going to let one person destroy this culture. I am not going to allow anyone to make my team take misery back to their families like that again. Never again.

The Feedback May Surprise You

Over the years, I have heard so many stories about people who let an employee go—an employee they thought would rock their organization because they were the "best" at their job, the one "no one could replace", but had a horrible attitude. I know we have all worked with someone who in theory was doing a good job, but couldn't work with anyone else and destroyed the whole environment. After they are let go, however, members of their team would come in the next day and say, "Thank you. I really appreciate you letting that person go."

No matter how much of a pace-setting person they were or how good they were at their job, their attitude didn't fit the culture. If their attitude destroys the culture, the rest of the team will thank you for letting them go and protecting the culture they love.

The Eagles will come in, step up, and rise up to the occasion, and they will do it amazingly quickly. They will realize what you just did, and that you took the hard step for the good of the team. They will walk through fire for you. This is what a Super Culture™ creates.

The bottom line is if you are not prepared to get rid of your turkeys, then your Eagles will fly off to another company for a small increase in pay. But turkeys don't have options to go to other places, and they will be with you forever if you let them stay!

THRIVE

Setting Goals and Rewarding

Through setting and hitting goals and rewarding, Super Cultures™ do thrive.

Set clear goals every quarter based on the one-year vision document. In my company with a Super Culture™, a CEO, manager, lead, direct report, or whoever the leader is sets the goals most of the time. I think most companies should set quarterly goals, and sadly, most do not.

Companies should have three major goals a month. There can be several minor goals to drive the major goals and how to accomplish them, but three major goals are what the entire company should focus on. More than three major goals in a quarter, and your team will lose focus.

Goals should be posted in an area where everyone on the team can easily view them. The goals should also be updated daily if possible and at least weekly. This gives the team a scoreboard to know when they are winning or losing. Could you imagine turning on a football game in the 3rd quarter with no scoreboard? You would quickly lose interest. A corporate team will quickly do the exact same thing.

Example: Let's say there is a retail jewelry store and they want to specifically increase watch sales. You could have a new watch sales goal of 100 watches per quarter. There could be 10 different new watches that drive it. So, the total of any 10 watches leads to one overall sales goal. So, the team gets educated on all 10 styles and features of the 10 watches you have. Any combination of the 10 minor items (in this case, watches) leads to the overall sales goal that you track.

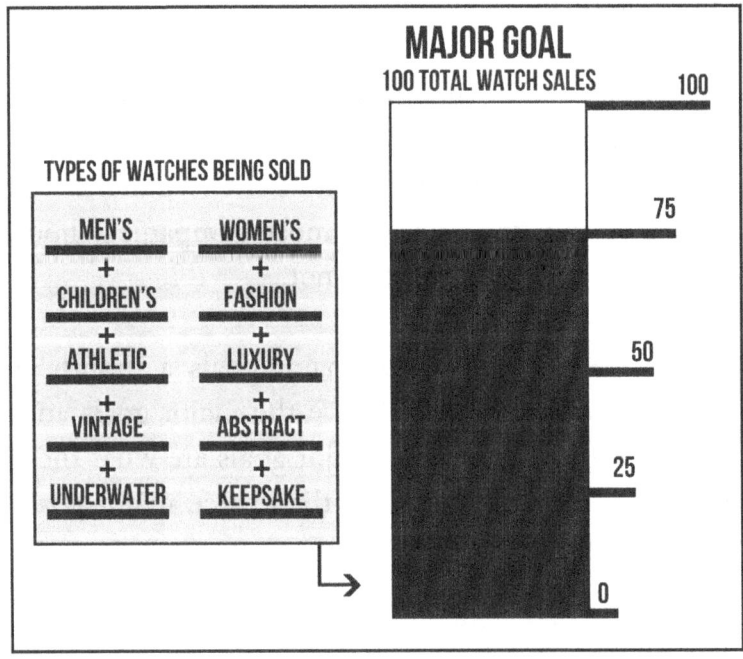

Super Cultures are always growing and thriving through setting goals, praising, and holding accountability. There is no balance; you are always either growing or shrinking.

What Thriving Looks Like:

- Every document is always getting better, clearer, and stronger.
- Praise is constantly going up.
- Leadership is always growing.
- Emotional intelligence is always growing.
- New goals are set in bigger vision documents and achieved.
- New and better processes are created.
- Teamwork is enhanced.
- More problems are solved.
- An environment of greatness is achieved.
- People feel appreciated and take pride in their role.

Rewards

Sometimes companies can't give a cash bonus, but I think you can at least give praise as a reward or celebrate with pizza or deli day, employee recognition, a special parking spot, or time off. I like to play games to keep things fun. I've created a poker game, a Bingo game, and The Most Memorable Moment, March Madness, Olympics, Lottery, and several others. We track things so we can praise on a daily basis and so we can hit big outstanding goals. This creates championship moments. Eagles want challenging goals (we talked about dopamine, noradrenaline, and oxytocin leading to acetylcholine in Chapter 3).

In most Normal Cultures, there is no goal setting, so the job gets monotonous. You go in. You do your job. You have no sense of why. Managers don't even know what to praise because there was no visionary-style leadership to even set a goal for the quarter.

In Normal Culture, You Lose Eagles—You Lose Sales.

Now that we have described all 5 Simple Rules to create and maintain a Super Culture™, let's start your journey to making one with the next chapter.

To download templates and resources for this chapter, visit www.chriscornelison.com or scan the QR code at the back of the book.

Key Takeaways

✔ **Hiring the Right Fit for Super Culture™:** It's not just about finding someone with the right skills; they've got to fit the culture too. By using position agreements and your Super Culture™ document, you'll ensure the people you bring on board align with the goals and values of your company. Don't rush the process—take your time to find someone who's the right fit.

✔ **Training That Lasts Beyond Day One:** Most employees start strong in that "honeymoon phase," but they'll fizzle out if you don't keep training and giving feedback. Keep the momentum going with regular check-ins on days 8, 15, and 30. This keeps them growing, keeps them focused, and prevents them from slipping into mediocrity.

✔ **Firing to Protect Your Eagles:** Firing someone is never easy, but it has to be done if they're dragging down your culture. You can't let a turkey bring down the Eagles. Protecting the culture means you sometimes have to make tough decisions to keep the environment thriving for your top performers. Eagles won't stay if you keep letting turkeys roam free.

✓ **Setting Goals That Keep You Winning:** Super Culture™ thrives on clear goals that the whole team knows and tracks. Set three major goals every quarter, and make sure they're visible so everyone can see the progress. When the team knows what they're aiming for, they're much more likely to hit the target—and then some.

✓ **Recognizing and Rewarding the Team:** You don't have to break the bank to show appreciation. Whether it's a simple "thank you," a pizza day, or a fun game to keep things lively, recognition keeps your team motivated. People want to feel appreciated, and rewarding their hard work ensures they keep bringing their best every day.

CHAPTER 8

Maximizing Your Business Success!

"It all seems impossible....until it is done!"

~Chris Cornelison

Now that you have the 5 Simple Rules to create a successful environment and a happy team, which I call Super Culture™, it is time to decide where to start.

On your journey to creating a Super Culture™, so much is possible—much more than you imagined. Anything that can be written in the vision can be accomplished in a Super Culture™. Creating a better work environment unlocks the ability to create bigger and better solutions to problems. For your company, that may mean mergers, acquisitions with other companies, big growth strategies, inventions, immense happiness, pride, better processes, and longevity for all. The sky's the limit of what you can accomplish.

Perhaps your Super Culture™ unlocks new marketing and sales initiatives because you have newfound capacity and energy. All these things can happen when you create a culture that inspires leadership and teamwork because it allows your people to be happy and thrive. So, let's explore some ways to put these 5 Simple Rules into play.

What Now, or How Do I Get Started?

One way you could get started is with your vision. Go to www.chriscornelison.com and get a free template and instructions to help you write down exactly what you want. A QR code is in the back of this book for easy reference.

Then, write your Super Culture™ Document; Chapter 2 will remind you how. It can be as short as 3 lines or as detailed as you want. I strongly suggest 1-4 lines at the most for your first one because the key is actually honoring what you write down, not just having a nice document. Remember, you can update the Super Culture™ document anytime.

Then, decide what you need to improve for the next quarter "personally." **IT ALL STARTS WITH YOU.** This can be as simple as saying "good morning" to everyone on the team every day for 90 days.

Then, pick 1-3 goals for your company for the next quarter based on your vision. If you are currently not setting any goals, maybe you just pick one goal, and make it simple. Maybe it is to sell 30 of a new product next quarter. Or perhaps the trash isn't taken out daily, and it is an issue for you, and you want it fixed. The goal becomes "take out the trash every day for a quarter," and you track it every day for 90 days. Goals can start as small as everybody sharing one positive comment from the previous day and get as complex as increasing by $1 million in a calendar year.

Then, you must make sure the team has the resources, training, and anything they need to hit those goals. No goal can be hit without these. Everything rises and falls on leadership, praise, and accountability.

Then, Praise What You Want Repeated™ EVERY DAY. Praise 10 times minimum per day and give the "whys" when you praise.

Hold accountable anything that doesn't honor the written down goals, vision, and culture, and give the "whys" when you hold accountability.

Track the goals and daily wins, and celebrate the big wins at the end of the quarter.

Repeat these steps every quarter and thrive forever.

It all starts with you...and it all ends with you.

Your team's improvement starts with you. Can you serve them, allow them to become better leaders and higher achievers, and teach them to praise what they want repeated?

If Putting It Into Play All At Once Seems Overwhelming, Take It Slower.

Maybe you just decide to work on yourself for a whole quarter. Maybe you decide to quit getting mad every time something goes bad. So, you focus for 30 days on being "emotionally aware" of what makes you go into amygdala hijack and 30 days on gaining "emotional control," and instead of getting mad, you pause, allowing yourself to think, and problem-solve a better way to do things so it doesn't get to the point shutting yourself down. Then, you spend the last 30 days of the quarter practicing "emotional improvement" and implementing a better process to make the problem go away.

Maybe you just pick one sales goal for a quarter and train the team on how to make the sales. You get a Praise Coin for you and all your leaders. Focus on praising anything that executes the sales for the next 90 days. Therefore, you really have 2 goals: increase sales and increase team praise...which improves culture!

The only way to fail in starting to create your own Super Culture™ is to not do anything at all.

Some of you reading this book will already have a successful company but aren't hitting goals and need a little cultural improvement. You may be ready for what I call the Million Dollar Bag of Coins™.

I've created an implementation tool I use in my companies, which many others have used over the years. Let me introduce it to you and show you how it can help you motivate your teams to hit more goals.

Million Dollar Bag of Coins™

I use an implementation process called the Million Dollar Bag of Coins™. It's a fun tool to use month after month that helps your team implement new processes and goals.

There are three keys to implementation: Leadership, Praise, and Accountability. Any time you take on a new goal, the Million Dollar Bag of Coins™ can help motivate and focus your team. Let me show you how they work and give you a brief example.

Leader Coin

The Leader Coin encourages the person with it to be a good visionary and servant leader by asking, "Have I given my team the resources (education, materials, training, etc.) and a clear goal they need to succeed?"

- Whoever has the Leader Coin should check the goal daily for the first 30-90 days.
- The holder of the Leader Coin should be serving, praising, and coaching.

The number one job of the leader is to clearly show the vision and direction of the company. The Leader Coin encourages leaders in all departments and on all levels to meet their goals.

Praise Coin

This coin is meant to Praise What You Want Repeated™.

- Whoever has the coin is reminded to use coaching leadership to lead their team to hit the goal.
- This coin reminds the person carrying it to praise things that lead to the goal at least ten times a day.
- This coin often can be passed among several people who need to praise what they want to be repeated.
- The Praise Coin is often held by the manager or project lead.

Several members of your team have the duty of praising things you want repeated in your culture. These coins remind them to praise anything someone does that takes them a small step closer to an active goal.

Accountability Coins

These coins go to the pacesetting leaders who will interact with your customers and lead you to your goals. Each coin says "Accountability" and challenges them to be accountable to the goals we have set. It could be accountability for asking for a sale, executing a new process, or choosing a great attitude toward the goal and giving a corresponding action to it.

> **NOTE: It is impossible to give a team member an Accountability Coin if the Leader Coin holder hasn't clearly set a goal and offered the resources to achieve the goal.**

- These coins get passed out to the team.
- They're told how or where to turn them back in.

This coin holds the team accountable to educating one to ten customers a day on the things that lead to hitting your goals.

- Accountability Coins remind the carrier to focus on ten actions per day, going toward 3 main goals for the team.

These coins are in different colors and can be used for specific departments or as ways to track which employees are executing the best.

The ten Accountability Coins can be stacked, and people can move them as they accomplish tasks. Or, they can be given out to team members to put in their pockets and turned in when they have completed the daily tasks assigned to the coin. The leader may then ask what happened that day and praise the steps the team members made toward the company goals.

I like having a team so strong that I just pass out all ten Accountability Coins, choose 3 goals, and encourage them to use their expertise as an employee to complete one action toward a goal.

This bag of coins creates a fun way to hold Leadership, Management, and Technician Levels on the organizational chart accountable to the goals by serving as daily reminders. The management level passes out coins before every shift for 90 days, and it becomes a fun way to hold the implementation of goals accountable.

How Does This Look In Action?

We will explore what using the Million Dollar Bag of Coins™ looks like in a work environment.

Let's create a restaurant called "New Super Culture Restaurant." Let's say they read this book and decided to go to the website and follow the 1-year Vision Template (or wrote one in my 2-day Super Culture™ class). In the vision, they wanted to increase revenue by $100,000, improve the dining experience, and improve company culture.

The first goal that is set to help the team reach the $100,000 increase for the year is to focus on increasing dessert sales. The staff is trained on 3 new desserts, and a picture of the desserts is placed on the front of the menu. The process is changed for servers to remind diners to save room for one of the new dessert selections, bring out examples of the desserts on the last visit to the table, and ask them to try our "Famous City Dessert Trio."

We add *"smile and welcome every customer"* to our Super Culture™ restaurant process of serving the table. This may sound simple, but our Normal Culture didn't have this process on the position agreements.

Now, the leader has to train the team and management on the new processes and how to manage the team for accountability. The leader sets the quarterly goal for the new desserts to be 750 sales (250 sales per month). The restaurant is open 25 days per month, which comes to 10 desserts per day to hit the goal. The person holding **the Leader Coin** places the goal sheet in a visible location for the employees.

The leader gives every shift manager **a Praise Coin** and directions to praise all the little things the servers are doing well. For example, learning the new process, remembering to ask on the front end to save room for dessert, using the new name "Famous City Dessert Trio," asking after the meal, and making the sale.

Everyone on the shift gets **an Accountability Coin** to remind them to ask these questions at their tables. They report back at the end of the shift how many they sold, what went well, and what needs fine-tuning by the manager. The manager immediately praises all of those fantastic contributions.

Leadership adds the processes, management trains servers to do it, and we track it on the goal sheet by all 10 accountability coins coming back in every day.

Lastly, a 1-2 minute huddle happens daily to track results.

Huddle Example

Yesterday was Day 1, and we sold 12 desserts: "Sarah had a great experience and actually sold 4 desserts to one table. Sara, would you share?" Sara then tells how she had a large table, and they bought 4 desserts to share between 8 customers. We praise Sara, and everyone gets a chance to accomplish that during tonight's service.

We are on track to hit our goal already. Someone shared a good experience that a smile and a welcome created. Jake says, "I smiled at people and noticed they smiled back. After a warm welcome, they actually really enjoyed me telling them about our City Famous Dessert Trio."

We praise Jake, give him a high 5, pass out new Accountability Coins, and tell everyone to keep up the good work tonight! Everyone gets a fist bump for the team's success from yesterday. The team feels successful, the team feels appreciated, and the customers are having a great experience. Our culture is growing!

Restaurant Super Culture™ is well on its way to hitting the goal for the quarter.

To purchase the Million Dollar Bag of Coins and download the instruction template or sign up for a training class, go to www.chriscornelison.com.

Next Up:

Let's look at how a Super Culture™ works in an athletic coaching environment. In the next chapter, I dive into how this framework empowers athletic teams to create a Super Culture.

Key Takeaways

- ✔ **Write the Vision and the Culture Document:** Everything starts with a clear vision. If it's not written down, it doesn't exist. Keep the Super Culture™ Document simple but real—1-4 lines max. The key isn't in writing a fancy document; it's in sticking to it.

- ✔ **Don't Overthink It, Just Start:** You don't need to change everything overnight. Pick one goal, get your team the tools they need, and praise the effort. Progress is progress, even if it's small. Super Culture™ is built brick by brick.

✓ **Million Dollar Bag of Coins™ for Results:** The Million Dollar Bag of Coins™ makes implementation easier. The Leadership Coin makes sure goals are clear, the Praise Coin drives daily recognition, and the Accountability Coin ensures action. It's a fun way to keep everyone locked in on the goal.

✓ **Track the Wins, Celebrate Often:** Set clear, visible goals. Track them every day and celebrate the victories, big or small. When people know they're winning, they keep pushing for more.

✓ **Consistency is King:** Set new goals every quarter, praise daily, and hold everyone accountable. It's a cycle—keep it going, and your Super Culture™ will grow stronger with each quarter.

CHAPTER 9

Implementing Super Culture™ As A Coach

I wrote this book with entrepreneurs, CEOs, managers, governmental employees, and workplace leaders in mind. But it can be used in just about any setting with a daily environment. For example:

- Parenting
- Church
- Government
- Social Organizations
- Non-profits
- And your life in general

I love athletics and am especially drawn to teachers, schools, and coaches. My son is currently in college to be a teacher and coach. I love the quote, "A coach affects more people in a year than most people do in a lifetime."

Chris Cornelison is one of the most dynamic speakers an organization can get on motivation and leadership. He will simultaneously have the crowd entertained and learning. He did so great for the Mississippi Association of Coaches we brought him back for a second year!

Coach Richard Russo
President of the Mississippi Association of
Football Coaches

An athletic culture is not much different than a business culture.

The 5 Simple Rules Still Apply

In most programs I've been around, there's usually something written on the locker room wall or similar area—a mantra representing their culture. For example, Coach Chip Bilderbach, who led his team to the State Championship at Columbia High School in Columbia, MS, had this on his locker room wall: "Success isn't owned. It is leased, and the rent is due EVERY DAY!" Having this visible serves as a daily reminder to his athletes that consistent hard work is expected. When a team puts its values and goals into writing, it helps to hold everyone accountable.

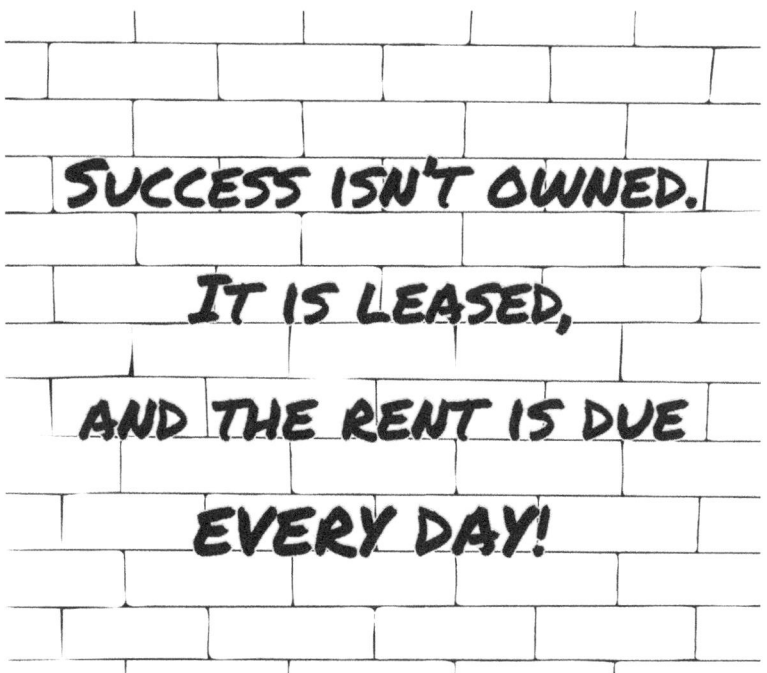

Coach Bilderbach would give an award of a yellow hard hat, take athletes' pictures in front of the wall, and make a social media post about what the athlete did to earn the honor. How hard do you think his players worked at practice to earn that honor?

It's important to note that an athletic culture can be outlined in a document emphasizing the point, "We strive to win the game." For example, if winning is the goal and daily hard work is the expectation, then the document would state, "We do what it takes in practice to win the game." A culture document can include a variety of principles and values that illustrate exactly what the environment of greatness standard is that will lead to accomplishing your goals.

Most people view athletic coaches as "great leaders," a perception that can be both accurate and misleading, often shaped by the visible success or failure on the field. However, coaching goes beyond this simplistic view. Coaches often employ a command and control style, such as yelling at players and driving them forward, which can be necessary in certain situations. This approach is particularly effective in high-pressure moments where quick decisions are crucial, such as in competitive athletics with limited time because of the clock. In these scenarios, command and control leadership highlights the need for decisive action and clear direction.

While this style of leadership can be very effective when used appropriately, it can also be counterproductive if applied in the wrong context. This is where I find common ground with coaches during our discussions. They appreciate the insights I provide about how the fight-or-flight response triggered by command and control leadership can impact their players negatively.

For instance, I explain that if a coach yells, "Chris, your practice was awful yesterday! If you can't do better, we don't want you out here!" right when I walk into the locker room, it could cause the player to go into an amygdala hijack, stop listening, and then they won't hear the great coaching advice you give when we break up for player meetings.

The clock wasn't running, and practice hadn't even started, so the situation wasn't time-sensitive; therefore, yelling or command and control wasn't necessary. You can definitely still hold me accountable for a horrible practice the day before, especially if you have praised me 10 times for things I actually did well. But the critical conversation now needs a coaching style of leadership, and that gives me the "whys" and teaches me the techniques I need to improve on and how to do better for myself and the team at today's practice.

Often, players get labeled as uncoachable, but the coach's understanding of emotional intelligence has a lot to do with how coachable an athlete is because it allows the coach to know when to use command and control leadership and when to use the coaching style of leadership. Obviously, the results in the team will go down, and the culture will go down if the only style used is command and control when the clock is "not" running.

I don't think it could be said better than Northeast Mississippi Community College Head Baseball Coach Richy Harrelson:

In this day and age, with technology and everything that is available to people, you are not going to out-coach many people anymore; so you better out-program and out-culture them.

~Richy Harrelson, Head Baseball Coach
Northeast Mississippi Community College

Coaches affect more people in a year than most people do in a lifetime

This statement is why I love coaches and teachers so much and why I love working with them. Kids need you! I often ask coaches, "Are you affecting them positively or negatively?" I honestly believe it is usually positive, but it's good to bring it to their attention that it can also be negative. The honor of being a teacher and coach is so valuable because often, that teacher or coach is all the leadership a young person will really see in their life.

Have you ever considered what happens if you use command and control at the wrong time every time you deal with a player? When your players go out into the workforce and try to use command and control as their only style of leadership, they will fail.

You need to realize that there are other types of leadership, such as coaching and visionary leadership, and they need to see those styles from you as well. Coaching leadership is not when you yell at them. Coaching leadership is when you teach them to perform their skills at a higher level and tell them "why" the hard work has to be done and "why" the skill needs to be done that way so they understand their role in helping your team win.

Positional leadership is why you "can" yell at them because you are the coach. They have to play for you at their high school. They don't have a choice to go somewhere else.

Misusing positional leadership and command and control leadership runs players off their teams. My goal isn't to make coaches feel guilty; it's to make them feel aware. I think that's why coaches resonate so much with what I have to say.

I help coaches become aware that there is a difference between Command-and-Control Leadership vs. Coaching-Style Leadership. I'd say a large majority of coaches and teachers are very caring and underappreciated people; this knowledge just helps them grow their environment and care for their players and students even more.

If you create an atmosphere of praise, set challenging goals, and hold people accountable, people will walk through fire for you, whether they are employees or teammates. The Super Culture™ will make every team a success, whether on the athletic field or inside the business.

As I mentioned before, my son is going to be a teacher and coach, and honestly, the day he told me was one of the happiest days of my life because of our shared love of athletics and how my respect for coaches and teachers impacts my own life.

Coach Jake Mills on lessons learned from Super Culture™

"Before discovering what emotional intelligence really was, my life was like a roller coaster. Up and down. I had a victim mentality that did not serve anyone but myself. Very selfish tendencies. After learning more and developing the ability to detach my emotions, I have really been able to prioritize the things that matter. So many things that made me upset did not matter. I became aware of the 'triggers' in my life. I had to understand the way I was feeling or making someone else feel was not right."

Jake utilized our Praise Coins with his team, and they helped in some surprising ways.

"I was so caught up in the BIG picture that I lost focus on the journey. Praise Coins allowed me to praise the things that are going to get us to our goals. My Praise Coin is either in my pocket or on our table in front of where I stand during our games for a reminder. Enjoy the ride, praise the small things."

Positive improvement in team relationships and performance spilled over into other areas when he adopted the Super Culture™ principles and made them part of his coaching routine.

"I think it's important to understand that it takes a conscious effort. This change does not happen overnight. It must be developed. Every day you must wake up and be aware of where you are mentally, physically, and emotionally. I am more focused on the things that truly matter. I am able to let the "noise" go. Our team is able to talk about a lot of topics that most teams cannot. They know they are able to come to me about things they are struggling with or do not understand. They also know they can come to me when they do

not agree with things within our program. It frees us up to work together, knowing we can trust one another."

Jake Mills, Head Baseball Coach, Petal High School

Empower Your Team

Whether your team is in the company or on the field, Super Culture™ enables everyone to perform at their best. Now, it's time to take a look at what your company looks like with a Super Culture™.

Key Takeaways

✔ **The 5 Simple Rules Work Anywhere:** Super Culture™ isn't just for the business world—it's for life. Whether you're coaching a team, leading a classroom, or running a nonprofit, these principles of leadership, accountability, and praise are what set great cultures apart from the rest.

✔ **Command and Control Has a Time and Place:** In high-pressure moments, like when the clock's running in a game, you may need to use command and control leadership to get things done fast. But it can't be the only style you use all the time, or it'll backfire. You can't motivate players or employees long-term with yelling and directives when there's no emergency or time-sensitive situation.

✔ **Coaching Leadership Builds Champions:** True leaders know when to switch to coaching mode. It's about teaching your team how to get better and giving them the "why" behind their work. When they understand their role and feel supported, they'll perform at a higher level.

- ✔ **Great Teams Thrive on Culture:** Just like in business, teams that focus on building a strong culture—where goals are clear, accountability is in place, and praise is consistent—are the ones that win. If you're a coach, it's your job to "out-culture" the competition.

- ✔ **Emotional Intelligence:** Makes Better Coaches: Being a great coach is about more than just knowing the game. It's about understanding how to lead people. If you can recognize when to push and when to pull back, you'll keep your players out of that fight-or-flight mode, and they'll be ready to give you their best every time.

CHAPTER 10

Your Company With A Super Culture™

If you change your thinking, you change your world.

~Norman Vincent Peale

It would be a shame if you read this book and thought, "I can't do this." It would be a shame to think that if you fail and stumble along the road to getting this right, you stop because there is no finish line to creating a Super Culture™. It is always about getting better; there is no right or wrong way to get there. This book gives you the guidelines for getting there, and it would be a shame if you never took the first step.

If you're not working on your personal emotional intelligence, you're not working on your leadership, and you're not working on your praise, that means everybody under you will be average for the rest of their life. And *you're* going to be average for the rest of your life. Let's take a look at a few people and how Super Culture™ has affected them.

Super Culture™ Success Story: Tim Douthit

The things I learned through the Super Culture™ training have helped me greatly. I learned that I and my employees could only improve and work on things with our jobs if we were taught and properly trained on how to do our jobs. For too long, I just expected my employees to follow by example the things I was doing at work and just learn by watching me. Yes, I know it's a terrible idea. The problem at Bendalls was that I would get frustrated with them when they did not do their job well.

The Daily Huddle meetings were very important and useful for discussing in 1-2 minutes the tasks or things important for that day and for praising someone for the excellent way they had done their job or were able to help someone. The example I can give is the joy I received by watching an employee's face light up when they were recognized for something extra or good they had done. The change that occurred with all the employees caught me off guard. When someone was praised, the other employees were truly happy for them, but the surprise was the self-motivation of each employee to do a better job and be recognized very soon.

The leadership training taught me how to empower my employees to be in charge of tasks in the pharmacy. In short, I slowly learned that I did not have to try to be responsible for everything at the pharmacy, which was not doing well at all, by the way. We went from a dictatorship to a democracy, so to speak. I also learned to have regular meetings with each employee to see how they were doing with their work and the jobs they did. I was able to learn about the issues that caused them pain or struggles. Actually, I learned to listen to the employee and ask some relevant questions during our discussion. But I also learned that the majority of the time, the employee was able to come up with a successful resolution to the problem on their own. The different ideas and tools I learned from Chris and Super Culture™ truly enabled Bendalls Pharmacy to change and improve how the pharmacy operated each day in all areas. I was able to begin the process of learning that people do not care how much you know until they know you care about them.

- Tim Douthit, Former CEO/Owner, Bendal's Pharmacy

Super Culture™ Success Story: Andrew Cannon

I mentioned to Chris that I attribute a lot of who I am as a pharmacist to various things I have learned from him over the years, whether it be in talks he has given, courses I have attended, or personal time I have spent speaking to him.

I think that one that stands out to me is the "it all starts with you" concept. I had my "garbage can kicking" moment about 10 years ago. I couldn't sleep due to the stress I was under as a new owner. I would often think that I had to suffer through 13 years of ownership until I could pay off the store and then, maybe, I could get myself some pharmacist help and get a day off. I would frequently go to the store early to clean up or catch up on the business side of the business.

One morning I was in a particularly bad place. I went in at about 5 am and started blasting Eminem. This is not the music I normally listen to, but it fit my mood that day. I was taking care of business. I had forgotten that one of my key employees was coming in early that day. When she arrived at about 7:30, she could hear my music outside of the building, loud and clear.

The whispers started swirling around the pharmacy, and everyone was terrified of me that day. They knew that I only listened to or played country music. Frankly, I was a little scared of myself that day. I think that I believed that it "all started with me", but only because I felt I was the only one capable of doing the work. It started, went through, and finished with me. I do not think that I understood what culture was or how I influenced it on a day-to-day basis.

Over the years, I have come to learn this concept and many more. The culture of my company has to be defined and written down. I have to embody that culture in the very way that I show up.

The good news is that I can CHOOSE my attitude. I have learned that I can empower my team. I have learned that I have stewardship over the lives of my employees, and it is my duty to send them home to their families in a better place than I found them. This is accomplished by praising their efforts.

We strive to be the best in the world and will work to become just that, but we appreciate our successes along the way. I have used the Praise Coins and had key leadership do it also, but the takeaway thing for me is that I should be praising 10 things before coming down with criticism.

Employees/spouses are like puppies. If you over-praise the behavior, the behavior will be repeated. That culture of praise has carried over to how my employees treat my patients. "Oh, you already have a probiotic, that is fantastic. Good decision! Now the way you are going to take it is 2 hours after each antibiotic and then daily for about a week after finishing your antibiotic." This reinforces the patient's behavior to take a probiotic and does not sound "salesy."

I try to close each day with a "thank you for your hard work" to my staff. We are implementing culture awards to be given out at our summer barbecue to praise those who live our culture. Most criticism that happens is a complement mixed with some coaching. "I really appreciate you bringing that solution to Mrs. Jones. Next time I would prefer you phrase it this way as I have come to learn it is more effective." One of the main jobs as a team member of each company is to bring up the spirits of those around you (patients, coworkers, vendors). Again, I hope you know how much you have meant to my career. Everything from the solutions brought to the example of consistency in Tuesday tips.

- **Andrew Cannon PharmD, CEO/Owner,**
City Drug Evanston, WY

Become A Better Leader

My hope is that no matter how big your dreams are, you have the courage to write them down and lead your team. My hope for you is that you accomplish every dream you reach for and you raise the bar higher each time.

My goal is for you to enjoy the ride of life along the way. Super Culture™ is about your day-to-day progress toward greatness. It's not about winning the Super Bowl on day one. That's not how it works. You change from day to day. You change the people around you by improving praise, holding accountability, and giving them a glimmer of light. You get better, and you make your team and environment better every day forever.

I hope that everything you dream about and everything you want times ten gets accomplished in your lifetime through the people around you because you create a Super Culture™.

Super Culture™ Success Story: Jade Schuckman

I believe every pharmacy owner has a great instinct to be successful and help solve their patients' problems. The problem is always getting your team on board to accomplish your goals. The takeaway from Super Culture™ that has helped me the most is this: It all starts with you.

If you are not reaching your potential as a successful independent pharmacy, you need to start by looking in the mirror. There is never a shortage of great ideas; there is a shortage of getting your team on board and trained to implement those ideas. I have hired numerous employees over the years who have no experience in retail pharmacy. When you train these individuals with the Super Culture™ concepts, you will turn them into rockstar employees who will be willing and eager to accomplish greatness. But as the independent pharmacy owner, you are responsible for creating and implementing the system in which these individuals can thrive.

- Jade Schuckman, CEO/Owner of Medicine Plus

Get Started Now

You can simply write down what you're passionate about, and create a Super Culture™ document. It's one page for me. **Four**

simple lines changed my life. It changes your thinking and lets everybody around you change, too. You see a bigger future, and it enables you all to go after it together. It raises praise. It raises leadership. It changes families. It changes lives. It hits goals.

When your company hits goals, everybody benefits. It creates pride.

The shame is in not doing anything if you read this whole book. You can pick the part you're most passionate about. Maybe you won't write anything down in the beginning and just praise.

But when you use all 5 Rules of the Super Culture™ roadmap, you possibly change thousands of people's lives. People you've never met—your customers, your team, extended family members of your team and customers, and most of all, your own life!

Why did I write this book?

I know this sounds cliché, but I am so grateful for the blessings my life has bestowed on me and my teams. I genuinely want to leave the world a better place while positively impacting as many leaders and people as possible. I love the concept of a Level 5 Leader in the book *Good To Great* by Jim Collins. A Level 5 Leader impacts people they have never even met. I hope this book allows me to be that Level 5 Leader who impacts leaders, companies, families, and work environments of people I may never even get the honor to meet.

I want to keep people from making the same mistakes I did. I want to help leaders who I have never met grow. I want to help create better work environments all over the world, I want to help people enjoy their jobs, and I want people and companies to be wildly successful!

Most people think I have a unique ability to coach and teach people in an understandable and usable way....I like to think of it as "next-level simplicity." I have been blessed to have had many, many mentors, and I have also had my fair share of failures along the way. My goal is to pay forward the lessons I have learned and hopefully save some people the hardships I have faced by giving them a better road map in the form of the 5 Simple Rules of Super Culture.

If you change your thinking, you change your world. And you change the world of countless others. I wrote this book because there was a time when I was miserable and hated my job, and that poured over into my personal life. Now, I love work, I love life, and I want to help others feel the same way about their work environment, job, and life.

I would love to help you on your journey. Please visit www.chriscornelison.com and choose one of my training classes or book me to speak to your organization about creating a Super Culture™. You can quickly and easily scan the QR code in the back of this book and get on track to a Super Culture™ in your own organization or team.

Key Takeaways

✔ **Take the First Step:** The biggest mistake is not starting. You don't need to have everything perfect from the get-go. Begin by taking action—whether it's improving your emotional intelligence, writing down your culture document, or just focusing on praising your team. The key is to get started.

✓ **It All Starts with You:** If you're not working on yourself, don't expect your team to improve. Your leadership, attitude, and emotional intelligence set the standard for everyone around you. If you want your team to grow, you have to grow first.

✓ **Praise Drives Success:** People thrive when they feel appreciated. Make it a habit to praise your team daily. It doesn't take much, but it builds a culture where people want to do their best. Praise what you want repeated, and you'll see your team's performance rise.

✓ **A Super Culture™ Changes Lives:** The impact of a Super Culture™ goes beyond just hitting business goals. It affects your team's personal lives, their families, and even your customers. Creating this kind of culture brings success, happiness, and pride to everyone involved.

✓ **Inaction is the Real Failure:** You don't need to master everything overnight. The real failure is doing nothing at all. If you take even small steps, like writing down goals or starting daily praise, you're already on the path to building something extraordinary.

Remember, this is about continuous improvement—there is no finish line, just a journey of getting better every day.

Conclusion

Reading this book isn't enough. Understanding the five rules isn't enough. You need to take action and implement the lessons inside this book before you can achieve Super Culture™ in your company.

In chapters one and two, I explained the differences between a normal culture and a Super Culture™. You learned that a Super Culture™ is a written-down and protected environment of greatness.

That environment of greatness means fun, love, leadership, accountability, and compassion both for you and your team. It means an environment full of opportunities to do more and be more. It means you can take a business from barely surviving to thriving.

People will look at your business as one of the best. They will want to achieve the level of success and happiness your company has, but will not be able to replicate your company's success. They don't have the 5-step roadmap that the five simple rules of Super Culture™ provide.

You Have The Roadmap

In Chapter Three, you learned **Rule 1: It Starts With You**. The path to an environment of greatness means you must change the way you think. You must realize that the number one thing a leader does is serve others. You also learned how understanding emotional intelligence helps you become a better leader.

In Chapter Four, you learned **Rule 2: Write It Down**. I gave you the five essential one-page documents every business needs to create a Super Culture™. Remember, if it isn't written down, it does not exist.

In Chapter Five, you learned about the power of praise with **Rule 3: Praise What You Want Repeated™**. We discussed how emotional intelligence works with praise to amplify team results and help your team achieve more goals.

In Chapter Six, you learned about **Rule 4: Hold It Accountable**. Accountability helps your team hit its goals by aligning leadership with accountability. Praising while maintaining accountability protects the culture by staying true to the company culture document's verbiage.

Chapter 7 gave you the last step in the roadmap with **Rule 5: Protect & Thrive**. Hiring, training, and firing procedures lift up and protect your company culture. I showed you how most companies fall into trouble during the Honeymoon Phase and how to keep it from destroying your culture.

You are fully armed to create a culture of greatness. You can create a Super Culture™.

The Choice is Yours Now

You can put this book down, not believe anything I've told you inside these pages, and do nothing. A Super Culture™ is within your reach. You have all the guidelines to get there, but you will never get there if you do not take that first step.

If you don't focus on yourself and work on your own personal emotional intelligence, you will never achieve an environment of greatness. Everyone under you will not recognize their full potential. You will have settled for being average.

I challenge you right now to write those four simple lines that will change your world like it did mine in chapter two. I challenge you to follow the 5-step roadmap of the Super Culture™ and change your life. You'll change the lives of those around you, and that's just the beginning.

You can change the world.

Every day, you will grow and move closer toward greatness. As you improve how you use praise, hold accountability, and use emotional intelligence, you'll help others grow. They will journey with you toward greatness, and together, you will all achieve more than you thought possible because you have Super Culture™.

Take all five steps of the Super Culture™ roadmap, and you have the ability to possibly change thousands of people's lives. Even people you've never met—your customers, your team, extended family members of your team and customers, and your own life!

Are You Ready For More?

Schedule Chris Cornelison as a Keynote speaker at your next company event or take a class from Chris. See how you can improve your work environment and get your team members on board with building your company's Super Culture™ by visiting me at www.chriscornelison.com.

It all starts with you....Now, what will you do next?

(Hint: I'd start with scanning the QR code)

About the Author

The Speaker:

Chris Cornelison has experience in leadership and business that most speakers can only talk about. His unique combination of humor and content will make you laugh and think. His high energy and engaging style motivate his audiences not just to consider making changes but actually to go out and do it. He has a fantastic record of creating high-performing teams and positive cultures. Whether he is speaking on the topic of culture or leadership, he is a speaker who will give you the tools to grow yourself and your business.

The Businessman:
A graduate of the University of Mississippi School of Pharmacy, Chris Cornelison owns several companies, including Solutions Rx, a multi-million-dollar supplement company he built from the ground up. As the former owner of three independent pharmacies, he was recognized as the Distinguished Young Pharmacist of Mississippi. He was voted PDS National Entrepreneur of the Year, McKesson Southeastern US Pharmacy of the Year, Tishomingo County Development Foundation Business of the Year, and won several Reader's Choice awards. Chris is a Who's Who in the Pharmacy industry. Chris also serves on the Northeast MS Community College Foundation Board of Directors. In addition to being a serial entrepreneur, he owns several exclusive formulas, Trademarks, and Copyrights.

The Person:
Chris and his wife, Janet, were born and raised in Iuka, MS. Chris is a 1989 Mississippi State Champion Baseball team member and played collegiately at Northeast MS Community College. Chris is still in the Mississippi high school record book for hits and stolen bases in a career. He has coached several elite baseball teams, including the Majors State champion, Team Mississippi. Chris is a devoted father to his son Alex and daughter Megan. If he isn't spending time with his family, which is most important to him, he loves watching, coaching, and participating in athletics. Chris avidly believes in giving back, evidenced by being heavily involved in several community projects. He lives his life in gratitude with a commitment to do everything he can to influence, grow, and help people improve their environments, companies, and personal situations.

Made in the USA
Monee, IL
08 February 2025

11767306R00105